The

Homeowners

Association

Manual

Family Subdivisions
Townhouse & Cluster Developments
Mobile Homeowners Associations
Master Community Associations

THIRD EDITION

Peter M. Dunbar, Esq.

D1445499

SUNCOAST PROFESSIONAL
PUBLISHING CORPORATION
P.O. BOX 10094
TALLAHASSEE, FLORIDA 32302

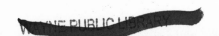

ABOUT THE AUTHOR

Peter M. Dunbar is a partner in the law firm of Pennington, Moore, Wilkinson & Dunbar, P.A., in Tallahassee, Florida. For a period of almost three years before joining the firm he served in the Office of the Governor of the State of Florida as General Counsel and later as Chief of Staff. Before joining Governor Martinez's staff, he was in private practice and specialized in the areas of real property and community association law. He has taught and lectured on associations and the law governing multi-family living since 1974. Mr. Dunbar is a member of the Community Associations Institute; he served on its National Board of Trustees in 1984. He was a Director and Vice President of Florida-Suncoast Chapter from 1980-1988. He is a member of the Florida Bar and an honors graduate from the College of Law at Florida State University.

Mr. Dunbar served as a member of the Florida House of Representatives for ten years. During his legislative career he served as a member of the House Judiciary Committee and sponsored or co-sponsored every major new law affecting community associations during his decade of service in the Legislature.

TABLE OF CONTENTS

CHAPTER 4
RULES OF PROCEDURE
AND PROPER DECORUM

CHAPTER 5
VOTING AND DETERMINATION
OF THE COLLECTIVE WILL

CHAPTER 6
THE BOARD OF DIRECTORS
OF THE HOMEOWNERS ASSOCIATION

CHAPTER 7
MEETINGS AND PROCEDURES
OF THE BOARD OF DIRECTORS

CHAPTER 8
OFFICERS OF THE ASSOCIATIONS

CHAPTER 9
COMMITTEES OF THE ASSOCIATION

CHAPTER 10
BUDGET, FINANCES AND INSURANCE

CHAPTER 11
AMENDING AND ENFORCING THE DOCUMENTS

CHAPTER 12
RIGHTS AND RESPONSIBILITIES
OF INDIVIDUAL OWNERS

CHAPTER 13
STYLE AND FORMAT FOR ASSOCIATION
FORMS AND DOCUMENTS

INTRODUCTION

The residents who assume positions of responsibility as officers and directors of homeowners associations will be the key to its success or the catalyst for its failure. The association is created to preserve the concept of planned residential living, and the officers and directors are charged with the responsibility of ensuring its success. These responsibilities can be significant and their implementation is governed by formal procedures that may be both new and confusing to community leaders.

Leaders of the homeowners association are, in almost all cases, volunteers and residents of the community. They are confronted with enforcing the covenants and restrictions among their neighbors and balancing community goals and the rights of individual owners.

The officers and directors carry out their duties within the formal confines of the governing documents, the rules of parliamentary procedure and applicable law. Collectively, these formal standards assure fairness and uniformity for community residents and present a unique challenge to the community leaders. The formalities prescribe notice and require open meetings. They establish eligibility and set standards of conduct for officers and directors, and they provide the methods by which the membership may express its collective will.

Formal policies and procedures do not have to be unnecessarily complicated and they should not frustrate the substantive goals of the homeowners association. This manual is designed as a practical guide to assist community leaders with their duties and responsibilities and as a reference tool to assure the successful operation of the homeowners association.

This manual provides a step by step explanation of the requirements for meetings, membership voting and the parliamentary procedures that govern gatherings of the association and its board of directors. It contains sets of forms and sample documents for use by community leaders and seeks to provide answers to the basic questions that arise from time to time on the operation of the community.

When officers and directors approach implementation of their duties, the author hopes that this manual will assist them and their advisors with problems of procedure and association organization. It is offered to simplify and clarify the formal and technical elements of association operation. By doing so, the main role of the homeowners association can be successfully carried out and the organization will function correctly for the benefit of its member-residents.

CHAPTER 1

UNDERSTANDING THE HOMEOWNERS ASSOCIATION CONCEPT

UNDERSTANDING THE HOMEOWNERS ASSOCIATION CONCEPT

Chapter One

1.1   General. The homeowners association is the cornerstone of a planned residential community. It gives continuity to the community, it preserves the architectural integrity and it maintains the common properties. Properly run, it promotes the community concept and protects the community's property values. In many cases, it makes available recreational and other facilities that might not otherwise be affordable or available to homeowners and residents. The homeowners association can be the vehicle for the community communication and security, and it can protect and maintain the common easements and common services that exist for the benefit of each member of the association.

Automatic and mandatory homeowners associations are part of an overall concept of residential property ownership. Purchase of the home or lot brings with it membership in the association which provides the structure for operation and management of the residential community concept. Membership includes certain mandatory obligations, financial responsibilities and a commitment to abide by the use restrictions and rules of the association.

The association's responsibilities may be limited to basic maintenance functions, or they may be expanded to include sophisticated and elaborate maintenance for the property and delivery of special services to individual homes. Association membership generally brings with it the obligation to pay assessments and the responsibility for each individual to contribute to the overall community well-being. To be successful, the community must be properly run by its officers and directors, and it must have some level of participation by each of its members.

1.2   Responsibility of the Individual Member. Members of the homeowners association have two responsibilities, one to themselves and to their individually owned property, and one to the association and the community concept. The individual responsibility requires the member to occupy, maintain and use the property in accordance with the restrictive covenants. By doing so, the member avoids the penalties and sanctions available to the association when enforcing the restrictions. By meeting the individual financial obligations, the member avoids the possibility of liens against the property and the levy of additional penalties and costs at the time delinquent assessments are collected.

The collective goal of the homeowners association is to maintain the quality of the property and the lifestyle envisioned by the planned residential development. Apathy by individual members can render the association ineffective and can destroy the community concept. To maintain the quality of life that accompanies a well-maintained residential community, each individual member must do his or her part. The success of the homeowners association will depend on how well each member meets and keeps the responsibilities that are established by the covenants creating the overall community concept.

1.3   **Interrelationship of the Parts.** The parts of a planned residential community consist of (1) the individually owned lots or residences, (2) the common scheme of covenants and restrictions that govern the homes and their occupants, and (3) the homeowners association that administers to the shared property and the community regulations. The parts of the community are melded together by the recorded restrictions. They encumber each individual lot or parcel of real estate and they impose their conditions, responsibilities and restrictions upon each lot owner. The recorded restrictions also grant membership rights in the homeowners association to each owner as an incident to the ownership of property in the community.

The parts of a planned residential community cannot be separated from one another once the covenants and restrictions are recorded and permanently encumber the parcels of property. Membership rights in the homeowners association are transferred automatically at the time that a piece of property in the community is transferred to its new owner. The covenants imposing financial obligations on each lot and restrictions on its use also remain with the property as a condition of ownership. The benefits of ownership are also transferred at the time of sale including rights to use the common property and the benefits from the common services.

1.4   The Law and Legal Principles. The corporate charter and bylaws for the homeowners association are established under the laws that regulate corporations in the State. These laws outline the full range of corporate authority and limits on that authority. The statutes establish the standards of conduct for officers and directors and provide for meeting and notice procedures that supplement the specific provisions contained in the association's governing documents. The State's corporate law will specify the annual filing requirements and filing fees necessary to maintain the corporation's existence, and it will set out the procedures for designating the registered agent and registered office for the association.

Traditionally, homeowners associations are corporations not-for-profit and the State's corporate law will prohibit distribution of any part of the corporate income to individual members, directors or officers of the homeowners association. The law does allow reasonable salaries to be paid to officers, directors and employees if the homeowners association's articles or bylaws permit. Under some circumstances, the association may be organized under a special statute such as the condominium, cooperative or mobile home act in the State. The special housing statute controls over general corporate law when there are inconsistencies between the two parts of the statutes.

Beyond the specific corporate law, the association must be sensitive to the constitutional standards that guarantee equal protection, due process of law and the right to contract to each association member. The declaration of covenants and restrictions is an elaborate contract among the individuals owning and sharing property in the community. Each owner is entitled to the protections which prohibit these contract rights from being impaired by others. Owners are entitled to defend their contract rights and to resist the efforts of those who would impair or take them away. The constitutional standards of equal protection and due process guarantee fairness and equality to each owner and member of the association. They prohibit discriminatory conduct by the association and arbitrary action of the board of directors. The association's operation must always be well within these constitutional principles if it is to be successful.

The board of directors must also be sensitive to the laws, ordinances and zoning at the local level of government.. Ordinances governing the health, safety and welfare of residents and the standards which govern the construction of buildings and improvements which serve them must be followed by the homeowners association. Repairs, alterations and modifications to buildings and other improvements maintained by the association must be done in accordance with local building codes. Other health and safety measures such as fire codes and restrictions on swimming and recreational facilities also restrict and guide the association's conduct and activities on behalf of the members.

Application of the law and legal principles to the homeowners association and to the planned community arrangement is not unnecessarily complicated. Each officer and director should be aware of its general requirements and should be prepared to call for legal advice from the association's attorney when assistance is needed on a particular point. Each homeowners association should have a legal advisor knowledgeable in the affairs of the community and the law applicable to it. When the board of directors and officers of the association rely on the attorney's advice for guidance, they have met their fiduciary responsibility to the association and will be relieved from any personal liability from adverse consequences arising from their action based on the professional advice.

1.5   The Declaration of Covenants and Restrictions. The declaration of covenants and restrictions is the document or set of documents that establishes the formal regulations for all of the property in the residential community. They restrict its use and govern the conduct and activity of its residents. The declaration of covenants and restrictions is the foundation document of the planned and well-ordered residential housing concept. The declaration establishes the basic rights and responsibilities for each owner, resident and guest. The restrictions and covenants grant easements and use rights to owners and guests, provide services and privileges to residents of the community and set the standards for maintenance and upkeep of all the property.

The recorded declaration imposes a greater degree of control on the rights of individual owners and the use they may make of their home and property than would otherwise be allowed if the restrictions and the homeowners association did not exist. When the declaration of covenants and restrictions is recorded, a quasi-government is created among the property owners when they become members of the association. As a member and owner, each individual must abide by the policies of the association and the conditions imposed by the restrictions.

The declaration of covenants and restrictions outlines the financial obligations of each owner and the rights which each owner has to take part in the affairs of the community. The recorded declaration creates the homeowners association, and generally the organizational document of the association is attached as an exhibit or is incorporated by reference into the recorded declaration. The impact of the covenants and restrictions is tempered by the right of each owner and member to participate in the affairs of the homeowners association, to select its leadership and to oversee its financial policies.

1.6 **Articles of Incorporation.** The articles of incorporation, or "corporate charter," is the document that formally establishes the entity responsible for maintenance, management and operation of the community property and the community concept. The entity is the homeowners association. The articles of incorporation provide the framework for the association's organization, define its membership and the voting rights of its members, and create the officers and directors who will act on behalf of the organization. The charter establishes the association's responsibility to administer to the shared community facilities and to promote and preserve harmony and uniformity within the residential community.

The term "articles of incorporation" includes the original document creating the association and all amendments to it and any other documents which define the existing form, membership and responsibility for the association. For example, the definition also includes articles of consolidation or articles of merger if several associations have been combined into a single organization. The articles may establish a corporation for profit or a corporation not-for-profit, but in most circumstances, the not-for-profit status is the alternative selected by the original organizers of the association. The articles of incorporation become effective and the homeowners association may begin to operate when the charter has been executed and filed with the appropriate state agency.

1.7 **Bylaws of the Association.** The articles of incorporation of the association define its basic structure and its areas of responsibility. The bylaws establish the procedures for carrying out these responsibilities. They define the powers and the manner for exercising those powers for the board of directors and by each of the association's officers. The bylaws create committees and describe how rules and regulations can be made and amended. Stated differently, the actual operation of the homeowners association is governed by the bylaws of the association.

Among the specifics traditionally found in the bylaws are the policies governing the use of proxies, the budget and finance procedures, and the qualifications and eligibility requirements for the officers and directors. Agenda and notice requirements for both membership and directors' meetings can be found in the bylaws as well as the dates for the annual and regular meetings. The bylaws may also set out the requirements for designating a voting representative when the property has multiple owners.

When the bylaws are adopted, there is a substantial amount of discretion available in the selection of alternatives to govern the procedures that will be followed by the association. Familiarity with the exact procedures is an important prerequisite to successful operation of the homeowners association.

1.8   Rules and Regulations. The supplemental restrictions authorized by the governing documents and promulgated by the board of directors are traditionally referred to as the "rules and regulations." The rules and regulations are similar to the restrictions and covenants contained in the recorded declaration, but they are not clothed with the same presumption of validity and enforceability unless they are also recorded as a part of the community documents.

The rules and regulations promulgated by the board of directors and not actually recorded can best be described as supplemental to the covenants and restrictions. These rules and regulations cannot contradict or contravene the provisions in the declaration or its recorded exhibits. The standard of reasonableness for rules and regulations made by the board of directors must be carefully applied to ensure their enforceability. To be valid, the regulations must be within the scope of the board of directors' authority as described in the association's governing documents.

1.9   Policy Statements and Resolutions. Statements of policy and resolutions of procedure outline and clarify existing standards of conduct for association members, property owners and their guests. They also establish standard forms for providing warning notices for violation of covenants or rules and as reminder correspondence to members late or delinquent in payment of assessments or management charges. Every community has some established policies and standard procedures for carrying out the regulatory functions of the homeowners association.

In many communities, "policy statements" and "resolutions of procedure" are not written or formally codified as part of the governing documents. To preserve consistencies in the community's policies and practices, these standard operating forms and procedures of the board of directors should be reduced to writing. The formal statements of policy and resolutions of procedure are then readily available for examination by all members and will ensure consistency in both practice and procedure from one board of directors to another.

Resolutions of procedure may provide for temporary assignments in the use of the common property, or they may include a procedure for reserving use of a recreation room or recreation hall. The range of subjects to be covered by policy statements and resolutions of procedure covers all aspects of community living. When the board of directors and the association take the time to reduce these policies and procedures to a written format, it helps to ensure that the procedures are tailored to the needs of the individual association and that they will be applied in a uniform, consistent manner for the benefit of all members of the association.

CHAPTER 2

MEMBERSHIP MEETINGS-
THE HOMEOWNERS' FORUM

Chapter Two

2.1   **General.** Membership meetings are an essential part of a successfully operating homeowners' association. The meetings provide a forum for association members to select their leaders, adopt and approve their financial policies, make changes in their governing documents, handle items of special business involving the membership and address other matters for the general welfare of the community. If proper procedures are implemented and followed, membership meetings can deal with the most controversial subjects and still end with productive results. Unless the association's bylaws otherwise provide, a majority of voting interests in the association must be present at a meeting to constitute a quorum.

In some circumstances, owners may take action by written agreement, without a meeting, when it is expressly permitted by the association's articles of incorporation, its bylaws, the recorded covenants affecting the property or the law requiring the action. In all other cases, actions requiring membership approval must take place at meetings that are properly called and conducted. The practices and procedures for conducting the meeting will be found in the association bylaws, the corporate law governing the homeowners association and the recorded covenants and restrictions affecting the property. The essential, traditional elements are highlighted in this chapter and throughout this manual.

2.2   **Annual and Regular Meetings.** All homeowners associations are required to hold at least one regular membership meeting each year. This meeting is referred to as the "annual meeting," and the date and time for this meeting will likely be set forth in the bylaws of the association. The primary purpose for the annual members' meeting is to fill the expiring terms on the board of directors, but often the annual meeting presents the only periodic opportunity that individual members have to review the affairs of their association.

A well-planned annual meeting will maximize the opportunities to provide information to the members of the homeowners association and to receive their input, suggestions and complaints. The bylaws for some homeowners associations provide for more than one regular membership meeting in each calendar year. The bylaws should be consulted to determine when the regular or annual meetings of members should be held, what business must be considered and whether more than one meeting is required in each calendar year. It is the responsibility of the officers and directors to implement the procedures for calling the regular and annual meetings of the homeowners association, and the bylaws will describe the necessary steps in more detail.

2.3   **Special Meetings.**   From time to time, members of the association or the board of directors may find it necessary to hold a special members' meeting.   Special meetings are limited in their scope and purpose, and in some circumstances a separate set of procedures must be followed when calling or conducting the meeting. The board of directors should anticipate, and be prepared to deal with, the special meeting procedures established in the community's documents.   In some cases, special laws such as a condominium or cooperative act will spell out definite procedures for the special meetings.   When the homeowners association falls into one of these special categories, the board of directors must be sensitive to these statutory requirements.

Community association leaders must always be prepared for the special needs of special meetings. In most circumstances, they grant special rights to members and owners, and proper procedures must be followed to protect the exercise of those rights. The bylaws will state who may call the special meeting and under what circumstances. In most jurisdictions, special meetings may be called by a petition of individual members of the association as well as by designated officers and directors of the association.

2.4   **Agenda and Order of Business.**   It is customary for each homeowners association to have a permanent order of business or "agenda". The required agenda for regular and annual members' meetings of most associations is specifically set forth in the bylaws of the association. The agenda for a special members' meeting should state the specific purpose for which the meeting was called, and the order of business will be limited to the special purposes that are set out in the agenda. It is advisable to provide a copy of the agenda to the membership at the time that notice of the meeting is given. The presiding officer of the meeting should follow the agenda correctly and should depart from the established order of business only if the rules of procedure for the meeting have been waived by a vote of two-thirds of the members present.

The order of business serves as a guide not only for the presiding officer but also for each of the members participating at the meeting. The agenda allows the meeting to proceed in order and for the presentation of business to be organized effectively under the control of the presiding officer. When the order of business or the agenda is not being followed, it is the right of any member to request that the proper order of business be addressed.

A member wishing to exercise this right may do so by calling a "point of order" and requesting that the chairman require the rules of procedure be followed. It is also the right of the presiding officer not to recognize any subject which is out of its order on the agenda or to terminate a presentation which is not part of the order of business under current consideration.

Agendas for most homeowners association meetings have items of both substantive and procedural business. The procedural items are customarily disposed of early in the meeting. "Calling the meeting to order" is done by the simple act of the presiding officer; the "calling of roll and certifying of proxies" is procedural and done generally without difficulty; and "proof of notice" can be handled by simply delivering the appropriate documents to the secretary of the association. In most cases, the procedural business items take little time while other areas of the agenda, such as the "election of directors," "unfinished business" and "new business" take up the bulk of the meeting's time and attention.

It is both desirable and advisable for the board of directors to consider creating sub-categories of the agenda where substantive business is to be discussed. Under the "election of directors," sub-categories may include (i) the report of a nominating committee, (ii) nominations from the floor, (iii) introduction and remarks by candidates and (iv) adoption of a resolution designating the number of directors. Under "unfinished business" or under "new business," sub-categories may include (i) matters relating to the budget and budget reserves, (ii) approval of modifications or alterations to the association property or recreation facilities, (iii) consideration of amendments to the community documents and (iv) other matters which the board of directors may wish to present to the membership for vote.

Agendas serve to prepare both the board and the membership for the business to be considered at the meeting and as a guide to carry out the meeting in an orderly manner.

2.5   **Conducting the Meeting.**   Conducting a fair and successful meeting is the responsibility of the presiding officer or chairman. The chairman must set and maintain the proper tenor for the meeting and, as chairman, must at all times be fair, impartial and neutral on each issue that comes before the meeting. The goal of the chairman should be to conduct an open and fair membership meeting without regard to the outcome on specific votes or motions.

In addition to setting an example of basic courtesy and fairness, the chairman must also be familiar with the proper parliamentary procedures used for conducting the membership meeting. By following proper procedures, the chairman can allow the meeting to proceed with full participation of all association members but without argument or disruption.

Debate or remarks by individual members should be limited or cut off only in extreme circumstances or when they are being made at an improper point in the agenda. It is not unusual to find one or more individual members who will attempt to be disruptive, either intentionally or because they feel strongly on a particular issue. In such circumstances, the chairman must remain courteous, patient and composed. The disruptive member desiring to be heard should be guided to the correct part of the agenda for his remarks and advised how to make them in an appropriate and dignified fashion.

Conducting a successful meeting requires the assurance that all members of the homeowners association wishing to participate can do so and that members wishing to make motions or debate an issue will have the appropriate opportunity. Particularly in large gatherings, it is helpful to have microphones available on the meeting floor to assist members wishing to participate.

The chairman should require members wishing to speak to stand or to come to the microphone and state their full name and their lot number or street address before beginning their remarks. This allows the secretary to identify the speaker for record-keeping purposes, and it introduces the speaker to the balance of the membership. If a microphone is not available, the chairman of the meeting should be prepared to restate the motions or the remarks for the benefit of all of the meeting participants.

2.6   **Reports.** The reports by officers and committees are often a part of the required meeting agenda and they provide an appropriate segment in the meeting for the membership to be updated on association affairs. Reports, however, may also lead to disruptive and unnecessary discussion if they are not properly presented and disposed of by the membership. Reports by officers and committees at the meeting should be basic summaries from written reports, and the written reports themselves should be available for separate distribution and a more complete analysis by members.

Reports of a general nature, including the treasurer's report, reports by social, recreational and other committees are, by their nature, informational, and unnecessary questions and remarks from the floor of the meeting should be avoided or deferred. Officers or committee chairmen should not request comments or questions at the conclusion of their reports, and if discussion is to be held on any portion of the reports presented to the meeting, it is appropriately brought up under the "unfinished business" portion of the agenda.

Occasionally, reports will require some special action by the membership meeting. Under such circumstances, the report should contain the specific recommendation being made, and it can be acted upon at the time that the report is concluded or under "unfinished business". Examples of such recommendations include reports by a finance committee, the board or the treasurer that the budget for the coming year be adopted or that expenditures for additions or repairs to the association properties be approved.

A report by the nominating committee recommending members for the board is also followed by meeting action. After receiving the nominating committee report, the recommended individuals are declared nominees by the chairman. Thereafter, the chairman should recognize other members desiring to nominate individuals from the floor of the meeting.

2.7   **Unfinished Business.** The unfinished business portion of the agenda is for the discussion and consideration of matters that have previously come before a meeting of the membership, either earlier in the present meeting or at a previously scheduled meeting. Business previously before the meeting under reports by officers and by committees and requiring membership action should be taken up and disposed of under this part of the agenda.

Such unfinished business may include the adoption of the budget, the establishment of the number of directors to serve for the coming year and other similar items of association business. To the extent possible, it is important for the board to identify, in advance, these matters of unfinished business. Items of unfinished business that can be identified in advance can be set aside under the unfinished business portion of the agenda as separate sub-categories.

The sub-categories will help to inform the members when specific items will arise within the general agenda category. The presiding officer will also be prepared to direct the members to the appropriate part of the agenda and maintain an orderly flow to the meeting. Unfinished business is appropriately restricted to matters previously before the meeting, and matters not previously on the floor should be deferred until the consideration of new business.

2.8   New Business and General Discussion.   The new business portion of the agenda obviously intends to deal with new matters not previously presented to the meeting. This part of the agenda is also the last or one of the last items to come before the meeting prior to its adjournment. As such, most required business has already been disposed of and more flexibility can be allowed by the presiding officer when permitting debate and discussion under the new business portion of the agenda.

Under new business, general discussion may be considered as an appropriate agenda sub-category. Additional tolerance and latitude can be allowed by the presiding officer towards the end of the meeting, and individual members can voice their objections or other concerns with association affairs at this time. In the unlikely event that the meeting and the discussion should become unreasonable and unruly, a motion to adjourn the meeting is always in order and can be voted upon without fear of leaving major items of business incomplete.

Other appropriate sub-categories of new business are items which require an extraordinary vote for approval by the members. Such items include proposed amendments to the community documents, approval of material alterations or modifications to the community property and other items where either the community covenants or the articles of incorporation or bylaws mandate an extraordinary vote. Again, the reason for holding these items for consideration as sub-categories under new business is the proximity of new business on the agenda to adjournment of the meeting.

The bylaws of most homeowners associations permit a meeting to be adjourned and reconvened if the required quorum is not obtained. An extraordinary vote can be postponed when an insufficient number of members is present to reach the required extraordinary majority. The business requiring only a simple majority can be disposed of first before the question requiring the extraordinary vote is placed on the floor. A motion can then be made to adjourn the meeting, after tabulating votes towards the extraordinary majority, to reconvene at a later date for purposes of counting the additional votes for the required extraordinary majority. While the new business portion of the agenda permits some creative options when seeking an extraordinary majority, it is important to consult the association bylaws for appropriate authority. The association's legal advisor should also be called upon to assist with the appropriate parliamentary steps. As under unfinished business, sub-categories for new business are recommended for an organized and complete presentation of the homeowners association business.

2.9   **Adjournment.** Adjournment concludes the proceedings and, in almost all cases, it occurs simply because there is no further business to come before the meeting. On rare occasions, a simple ending of the meeting may not be desired or may not be easily accomplished. Under such circumstances, the presiding officer must be prepared to deal with the unusual or unexpected. Since the motion to adjourn the meeting is the highest priority motion available from the floor, the presiding officer may need such a motion to be made if the meeting becomes disruptive or unruly. When made in its simplest form, the motion to adjourn is not debatable and is made and voted on before control of the proceedings is lost.

A different motion to adjourn will be used on occasions when the adjournment is to be followed by a reconvening of the meeting at a later time. Such a motion to adjourn and reconvene may be desired so that additional information can be brought to the membership or because the meeting has lasted for an excessive length of time and members are tiring. The motion to adjourn and reconvene may also be used when an item of business requires an extraordinary majority and an insufficient number of members is present to meet the extraordinary majority. The motion to adjourn and reconvene is debatable and, if made and approved, it will allow the meeting to be temporarily ended and reconvened at a later time for the purpose of continuing the meeting business and counting additional votes present at the reconvened portion of the meeting.

2.10 **Minutes and Records.** Minutes of the membership meeting serve as the permanent record of the proceedings. Their content should include a description of all pertinent items of business conducted at the meeting and the disposition of each item by the membership. A complete meeting record does not require that a word-by-word transcript be kept or that an elaborate account of debate and general discussion be placed in the written minutes. Proper minutes will confirm the time, place and presiding officer for the meeting. They will establish that proof or evidence of notice was given for the meeting, and they will state the exact quorum that is in attendance. These elements will provide a permanent record that a proper membership meeting was held.

The minutes will include an account of each item of business that was brought before the meeting and will contain a clear and concise record of the item's disposition. The use of exhibits to minutes provides a helpful way to organize a complete and accurate record of the proceedings. The proof or evidence of notice, copies of the notice and agenda, attendance and check-in sheets, reports and the actual vote tabulations can be included in the minutes by reference or as attached exhibits. Exhibits can eliminate lengthy minutes while maintaining a complete record of the meeting events.

In addition to the minutes and minute exhibits, there are other records from the membership meeting that should be maintained by the homeowners association. The certificates designating the voter representing a lot or parcel of property owned by more than one person or by a corporate owner must be kept and updated for continuing use at future meetings. The actual ballots and proxies which have been used during the membership meeting must also be kept by the association for at least one year.

When the minutes of the meeting have been prepared and approved by the secretary, it is advisable to make them available to the membership for inspection and review. This procedure will help keep the membership informed and will also provide a basis for the waiver of the reading of the minutes at the next regular meeting. The minutes of all meetings, and any records supplemental to the minutes, should be available for inspection by association members or their authorized representatives at any reasonable time.

CHAPTER 3

DOCUMENTS AND ORGANIZATION FOR MEMBERSHIP MEETINGS

DOCUMENTS AND ORGANIZATION FOR MEMBERSHIP MEETINGS

Chapter Three

3.1 General. The technical elements of a successful homeowners association meeting are not complicated, but they are important to the meeting's success. Proper form and format ensure that all members will receive notice of the homeowners meeting, that absent owners will be given the opportunity to register their preferences at the meeting and that the meeting will be convened and organized to allow the business of the association to be carried out fairly and in an orderly and timely way.

Forms and technicalities should never frustrate the ultimate goals of the membership gathering, but they are essential to a complete and proper meeting. It is the responsibility of the board of directors and the officers of the homeowners association to simplify meeting procedures. The leaders must ensure that the meeting will have a proper quorum and that each member wishing to participate in the decisions of the meeting may do so.

A proper business meeting of the association cannot be held without the presence of a quorum, and, unless the bylaws of the association establish a different number, a quorum will be a majority of the total membership. In order to successfully obtain a quorum, the membership must be notified and given an opportunity to properly participate at all formal gatherings of the association. It is the goal of this chapter to outline the basic procedural and organizational requirements that are necessary to ensure that success.

3.2 Notice and Proof of Notice for Meeting. A membership meeting cannot be properly held without notice or when notice has only been provided to part of the association membership. Under some circumstances, notice of a meeting may be waived, but members must do so in writing, and there must be authority for the waiver contained in the association's articles of incorporation or its bylaws. In addition to actually giving notice to all members, the board must also preserve evidence or proof that the notice was given to each of the association members in written form.

The giving of notice to members may be accomplished in one of two ways. The notice may be provided by U.S. mail to the member at the last address furnished to the association or it may be hand-delivered if the association member waives in writing the right to receive the notice by mail. To ensure that "proof of notice" is properly preserved, a little planning can go a long way. A roster of the current association membership should be maintained by the board of directors, and an extra copy of this roster can be used and can ultimately become the proof or evidence that notice of the meeting was given.

If the notice is to be given by U.S. mail, an officer of the association may provide an affidavit to be included in the association records stating that the notice has been given to each owner. The roster of members can be attached as an exhibit to the affidavit, and it becomes permanent and accurate evidence that notice was properly given. A certificate of mailing from the local postmaster can also be stamped on a roster of the members at the time that the mailing is left with the post office as evidence that notice was given. Finally, in a similar fashion, the roster can be used for the hand-delivered notices. Each member can sign adjacent to the name on the roster when the notice has been delivered. The roster, with owners' signatures, can then be used as an exhibit to the affidavit given by the officer responsible for delivering the notice.

The overriding concern in giving proper notice is to assure that there will be maximum membership participation at the meeting. It is important to remember that all meetings of membership are for the participation by the association members, and notice, or a waiver of notice, must be given or obtained from each member.

3.3   **Content of Meeting Notice.**   The notice for a membership meeting, whether annual or special, must contain the date, time and place at which the meeting will be held. If the meeting is a special meeting, the notice must additionally state the specific purpose for which the meeting has been called. In addition to the mandatory content for the meeting notice, other items may be included in the notice that are both advisable and helpful to the board and the membership.

These items include an agenda for the meeting, a voter designation or voting certificate, committee reports, a financial statement or budget, and a proxy for members who cannot be in attendance at the meeting. In a well-run community, the giving of notice will include, at minimum, the notice itself, an agenda of the business to be covered and a proxy form for the convenience of members who cannot attend in person. Additional items included in the notice mailing should be considered based upon the individual needs of the community. Notice of any proposed amendments to the community's bylaws or other governing documents is mandatory before they can be properly adopted. Proposed amendments should be part of the notice for any meeting where they are to be considered.

It is recommended that each homeowners association give a financial report to its membership annually. Including this report with the annual meeting notice can be both economical for the community and helpful to individual members. Its inclusion also permits discussion of the financial report at the membership meeting. If the budget is to be adopted at the meeting, or at a board meeting in close proximity to the membership meeting, copies of the budget should accompany the meeting notice.

As a final option, the notice can be accompanied by reports of committees, reports by the association's president or reports by the management company. If amendments to the community's documents are to be considered at the meeting, then copies should be included with the notice. It may also be helpful to include a general letter of explanation of the business to be discussed at the membership meeting.

3.4   **Time of Notice.** The community bylaws will set out the length of notice required for the notice of members meetings in most circumstances. If no time is established in the bylaws, it is good practice to provide at least two weeks (14 full days) written notice prior to the meeting. To ensure notice is given timely, it is advisable to have the notices post-marked or hand-delivered prior to the day on which notice must be given.

Variations for the time of notice may result from the nature of the business to be discussed or the type of meeting being held. If a longer period of time is required for a special meeting or for special business to be conducted at a meeting by the bylaws, the board of directors should be guided by the bylaws provision.

Ample and correct notice to the association members is a procedural prerequisite to a valid membership meeting.

3.5   **Proxies.**   The bylaws of most homeowners associations permit absent lot owners to participate and vote in membership meetings by proxy. The corporate statutes in most jurisdictions also authorize and permit the use of proxies by a member but place limits on the use of proxies under certain circumstances. Condominium and cooperative associations often have special requirements and restrictions placed on them by statute. A complete membership meeting mailing by the board of directors should include a blank proxy for the proposed meeting. The proxy may be general in nature or very specific, limiting the person designated to vote it and allowing little discretion when representing the absent member. A limited proxy is similar to an absentee ballot and is used to direct the absent member's vote in a specific way or for a specific candidate.

To be valid, the proxy should identify the person who will vote the proxy at the meeting. The identification may be made by name or by designating a specific officer of the association such as the president or secretary. The proxy must identify (1) the meeting for which the proxy is given, (2) the membership interest which the proxy represents, (3) the member who is granting the proxy, and (4) it must provide a signature block for all members of record or the voting representative to sign and date the proxy. The bylaws of most associations require that the proxies be returned to the secretary or other officer of the association prior to the meeting. Once the presiding officer has called the meeting to order, no further proxies may be accepted.

Unless the association bylaws limit the number of proxies which a single individual may vote, there is no restriction on the number that a member may vote. A proxy may be revoked at any time by the member giving it prior to or at the membership meeting. A power of attorney may be used as a proxy if it contains all of the required proxy information and it otherwise meets the legal standards and restrictions required for a valid proxy. Unless the bylaws specifically require otherwise, the person designated by a proxy does not have to be a member of the association, and a member may designate a renter, his attorney or another non-owner to represent the unit.

3.6   **Designation   of   Voter.**   The bylaws of many homeowners associations provide for the designation of a voting representative for the lots, units or parcels which have multiple owners, or which have corporate owners. The "voting certificate" or "designation of voter form" is sometimes overlooked by the board of the association and is often confusing to association members.

Failure to have such a voting certificate on file with the homeowners association is the most common reason why a membership interest is not permitted to participate at a membership meeting, especially when an election issue is close and proper procedures are being closely followed. The bylaws of the homeowners association should be consulted for the need, the content and the persons who are eligible to be named in the voting certificate.

A voting certificate form should be on file in the association records from each jointly-owned and each corporate-owned membership interest in the community, and a roster of "designated voters" should be maintained by the association secretary. The voting certificate remains valid until the owners wish to change the designated person or until the property is sold.

Unlike a proxy, which expires upon final adjournment of the meeting for which it is given, the term for the voting certificate is indefinite. The joint ownership by husband and wife should not be overlooked and a designation should be made by them as well. When selecting an individual to be the designated voter, it is advisable to select one of the owners of the membership interest to serve in that capacity, if possible. Corporate owners should select an officer of the corporation owning the lot, unit or parcel.

While the form and content of a voting certificate and a proxy are similar, they are designed to serve different purposes, and, in most cases, one document cannot be substituted for the other.

A voting certificate cannot serve as a proxy if it does not identify the specific membership meeting at which it is to be used and if it survives for a period beyond the meeting's final adjournment. A valid proxy by multiple owners may, on the other hand, serve as both a valid proxy and a valid voting certificate for a specific meeting. If the proxy has been signed by all of the owners of record and if it appropriately designates a voter, the proxy may serve the dual purpose for the meeting at which it is presented. Upon final adjournment of the membership meeting, the proxy would expire, and it would not survive as a voting certificate for future meetings.

3.7   Check-In Procedures. Proper check-in procedures help to ensure an orderly and successful membership meeting that will begin on time. The initial key to a successful check-in process is a current roster of members and a current roster of designated voters. When the appropriate rosters are available, the proper meeting participant can be easily identified and admitted to the meeting with the appropriate voting ballots. To ensure complete and proper participation in the meeting, accountability for the voting membership must be ensured at the time of check-in to the meeting place.

Controlled entry of voting members enhances a successful check-in policy. Depending on the size of the homeowners association and the number of voting members, a predetermined division of the community should be made. The division or classifications, by lot or parcel number or by alphabetical order, should be made so that an appropriate number of check-in stations can be established. Each station should have a roster for members and designated voters to confirm ownership and the voting representative for each lot or parcel. A balanced division of lots or parcels by number or by alphabetical grouping helps to avoid delays and allows each member to be admitted to the meeting so it may begin on time.

Effective check-in procedures will also allow for distribution of ballots to designated voters at the time of the check-in, eliminating the necessity of distributing ballots once the meeting has commenced. To ensure that ballot distribution at the time of check-in is successful, it is important for the board of directors to anticipate the contested issues that will come before the meeting and to have a ballot prepared which will address each issue appropriately.

3.8   Presiding Officer Selection. Selection of the proper individual to preside at a meeting of the membership is an important ingredient for a fair and orderly meeting. In almost every community, the bylaws designate the individual who will serve as chairman of the meeting, or they will establish the procedures by which the presiding officer or chairman is selected. The bylaws may specify the officer, generally the president, or they may provide for the election of a chairman from the meeting itself. The bylaws may allow the president or the board of directors to designate a chairman for the meeting. In addition to these three options, it is also possible for the membership to select another presiding officer by waiving the rules and designating a chairman.

While most membership meetings do not have major elements of controversy, on occasion, controversial issues and closely-contested elections will arise. On such occasions, it is helpful to have an experienced individual presiding who is familiar with the issues before the meeting and the rules of procedure which govern the conduct of the meeting.

The presiding officer may not take part in the substantive debate, nor may the chairman make or second motions during the meeting. If the president, or other officer who would normally chair the meeting, wishes to participate actively in the debate and business, another individual must preside over the meeting. The presiding officer may vote by a ballot or may vote when the vote will change the results on the issue or break a tie. Otherwise, the presiding officer is not entitled to vote on issues at the meeting.

When the bylaws permit the board of directors to appoint an individual to serve as chairman, the appropriate resolution should be passed by the board prior to the meeting. If the bylaws do not specifically allow for a designation and the board still wishes to have a particular individual serve as chairman, the members can be asked to give their consent (for a waiver of the rules) to permit the individual to serve.   Under most circumstances, a properly presented request to the membership will be approved, and the desired presiding officer can assume the chairmanship of the meeting without controversy.

3.9   Pre-Meeting Preparations. For the presiding officer, the board of directors and other leaders in the community, an analytical review of the agenda and other procedural aspects of the coming meeting should always precede the meeting itself. The procedures which guide an annual meeting are not complicated, but they can be a trap for the unwary. With pre-meeting preparation, unexpected surprises and unnecessary delays can be easily avoided.

It is helpful to have motions written down and for the presiding officer to assign specific motions to designated individuals. By doing so, procedural items such as waiving the reading of minutes of the previous meeting can be disposed of orderly and efficiently. To the extent possible, the presiding officer should know who the nominees for the board of directors will be and who is going to nominate them from the floor. The presiding officer and the board should also anticipate points of difficulty and how such points will be dealt with, including the selection of sergeants at arms and, if necessary, appropriate outside security.

Pre-meeting preparation may include preliminary remarks by the chairman prior to formally starting the meeting. This is helpful particularly when unusual or complicated business is to come before the meeting. In such preliminary remarks, the presiding officer can explain what business is expected at the meeting, the manner by which a member can be recognized to speak at the meeting and at what point each item of business may be properly brought before the meeting. Brief remarks at this pre-meeting stage, and an assurance that all members will have the opportunity to be heard at the appropriate time, will often avoid shouting matches and major meeting disruptions during close votes or when controversial issues are being debated.

3.10 Recording and Taping Membership Meetings. From time to time, the board of directors may face a request or a demand by a member of the association to record or videotape the proceedings at a meeting of the membership. In some jurisdictions the law permits a member to record meetings in this manner as a matter of right. But even where no statutory right exists, the request to tape or record a meeting can be granted without unnecessary controversy or disruption with a little planning on the part of the association.

In anticipation of recording requests, the board of directors will find it advisable to have permanent policies that permit recording but regulate it in a fashion so that the activity does not interfere with the conduct of the meeting itself. Reasonable rules can appropriately require that equipment be installed prior to the beginning of the meeting at locations which do not disrupt the proceedings. Rules which ban equipment producing distracting sound and light emissions are appropriate.

Requests to record or videotape a meeting do not need to be intimidating to an association that is properly run. Membership meetings are for the benefit of the community and each of its individual members. Should a member wish to record a meeting, good practice dictates, and in some jurisdictions the law requires, that the member be permitted to do so under reasonable circumstances. A well-run community will anticipate these periodic requests.

CHAPTER 4

RULES OF PROCEDURE AND PROPER DECORUM

RULES OF PROCEDURE
AND PROPER DECORUM

Chapter Four

4.1**General.** Basic parliamentary procedure is nothing more than a set of rules to govern the conduct of meetings in a way that will allow all interested individuals to participate and be heard, and will permit decisions to be made in an orderly manner and without confusion. If the proper rules of procedure are followed, the meeting will be fair, it will protect the rights of individual members, there will be enough flexibility to deal with the full panorama of issues, and it will allow for a democratic result to be reached on each decision which comes before the meeting.

Every association needs to document its customs and the special rules that will govern the proceedings of the membership and the board of directors meetings. They can be tailored to the needs and desires of the association, but they should promote uniformity and basic fairness for the meeting and for those in attendance. *Robert's Rules of Order* (latest edition) is the basic manual used by many organizations, and it is frequently incorporated by specific reference into the bylaws of the homeowners association.

The uniform parliamentary procedures enumerated in *Robert's Rules of Order* and other parliamentary manuals will yield to the bylaws of the association when provisions are inconsistent. The meeting chairman must be familiar both with the general rules of procedure, and the specific variations of procedures contained in the homeowners association documents. While individual documents and individual community customs may dictate some variations in meeting practices, the overriding principles of parliamentary procedures are to ensure that fair and open meetings are used to carry out the business of the association.

4.2**Meeting Organization.** Meeting preparation is an important partner with parliamentary procedure. For a well-run community meeting, organization will consist of a pre-meeting checklist to ensure that notice has been properly given to all members, that a chairman has been or will be selected to preside over the meeting and that a secretary or recorder has been chosen to keep a record of the proceedings. The presiding officer of the meeting should have an organizational outline or guide prepared prior to the meeting.

The chairman's meeting guide will anticipate the business of the meeting, the motions and nominations which will be made and the individuals who will desire to be recognized to speak, make motions and submit nominations. A properly organized meeting will also anticipate the special needs which may arise from items of business on the agenda such as a blackboard for listing nominations and properly prepared ballots to ensure full membership participation in voting. If smoking is to be allowed, smoking areas must be appropriately designated. Meetings of homeowners and condominium associations are considered public meetings, and smoking restrictions will apply to association gatherings.

The presiding officer or the secretary should have a copy of the association's bylaws, the rules of procedure which govern the association's meeting and other community documents available for easy reference to deal with questions of proper meeting conduct when they arise. In addition to having these documents available, the presiding officer must also have a general working familiarity of them to ensure that they are properly applied during the course of the meeting.

4.3   **Motions and Seconds.** As the business of the meeting unfolds, subjects are introduced for consideration and vote by motions from the members present. Main motions introduce subjects for meeting consideration while subsidiary motions, privileged motions and incidental motions seek to modify consideration of a main motion or modify the normal course of the meeting business.

Limited informal discussion and questions about possible motions are sometimes beneficial and may be permitted by the presiding officer before insisting that a formal main motion be made by a member. The chairman should not permit the informal discussion to deteriorate into debate among members. When any member objects to the informal discussion, the chairman must rule it out of order and require that a specific motion be properly made and seconded if discussion on the subject being debated is to properly continue at the meeting.

As a general rule, all motions made by a member must have a second from another member at the meeting. The purpose of a second to the motion is to avoid wasting time when only one person has an interest in the subject of the motion, and others do not wish to discuss it. When a motion does not receive a second, the presiding officer will declare that the motion fails for lack of a second and proceed to the next main motion or order of business.

The meeting may consider only one main motion at a time. In order to make a motion, the member must first obtain the recognition of the presiding officer for the purpose of making a motion. If more than one member of the association wants to be recognized to make a motion, the chairman must select which member will be recognized. The motion is then stated to the meeting by the member who has been recognized. If the motion receives a second, then the presiding officer will state the motion before the meeting and declare that it has a second. Once made, seconded and stated, the motion is then in the possession of the meeting, and it cannot be withdrawn by the maker without the consent or approval of the meeting membership.

As a general rule, all main motions are debatable unless a motion to eliminate or limit debate has been adopted by a two-thirds vote of the membership present. After debate, the question is "put" to the membership for a vote. Once the results have been determined, the chairman declares the results on the motion, and it is then disposed of by the membership. It is then in order to make another main motion. Continued discussion of the motion disposed of is out of order unless a motion to reconsider is made.

4.4 **Subsidiary and Incidental Motions.** Subsidiary motions are those which are applied to other motions for purposes of modifying, amending, postponing or otherwise disposing of the other motions. Subsidiary motions are of higher priority, and they will supersede the main motion and must be disposed of before voting on the main motion. Examples include subsidiary motions to limit debate, amend the main motion or move the "previous question" on the main motion. An amendment offered to a document, report or other written instrument is technically an incidental motion and should be treated accordingly.

A motion for the previous question is made to halt further debate and is often misunderstood. It is a subsidiary motion, and it must be adopted by a two-thirds vote of those present before debate can be eliminated and a vote on the main motion taken. Unless a motion for the previous question or a motion to limit debate is adopted by a two-thirds vote, debate will continue until no one else wishes to be recognized. When no one else seeks recognition, a motion for the previous question is unnecessary.

Incidental motions may or may not arise out of another pending motion or question before the meeting. The incidental motions do not seek to modify or amend another motion but address how or when another motion or question will be dealt with by the meeting. Under most circumstances, an incidental motion must be disposed of first before consideration of a main motion can continue. Examples of incidental motions include motions to suspend the rules, motions to close or reopen nomination, motions to divide a question before the meeting or motions to waive the rules. As a general rule, incidental motions are not debatable and cannot be amended by the meeting.

4.5 **Privileged and Unclassified Motions.** Matters of privilege and privileged motions do not relate directly to pending questions before the association meeting. Matters of privilege are considered of the highest importance to the meeting and the conduct of the meeting itself. Motions of privilege take precedent over all other questions before a meeting, and they must be disposed of before further business can be conducted. As a general rule, motions and matters of privilege are not debatable once they have been made and seconded.

Examples of privileged motions and matters include motions for adjournment, motions to recess, demands that the meeting conform to the proper order of business and questions or privilege claimed by an individual member for himself or on behalf of the meeting. When seeking the floor for a motion of privilege, a member follows the same procedure for making any other motion. When seeking the floor on a matter of privilege, a member will state that he wishes to take the floor on a point of personal privilege or to state a point of order.

There are some motions which are not classified in the other groupings due to their unique nature or because they may be applied to a motion in one of the other categories. Unclassified motions include dilatory and frivolous motions. The presiding officer may choose not to recognize or may rule out of order these types of motions because they abuse the rules of parliamentary procedure and delay the proper course of the meeting business.

A motion to ratify an act previously done by an officer, the board or committees of the board is also an unclassified motion. A motion to ratify can be approved only if the act could be properly done if authorized in advance by the meeting membership. A motion to ratify a previous action is generally used to cure a potential procedural defect in the act or when there is a question concerning the limits of authority when the act was originally taken by the board. As a general grouping, most privileged and unclassified motions are not needed during most meetings, and they are used only on infrequent occasions.

4.6   **Reconsideration.** The most common of the unclassified motions is the motion to reconsider. It is also the most frequently used unclassified motion, and it can be made relating to any motion previously adopted in the meeting. A motion to reconsider the vote on a motion is debatable if the motion it seeks to reconsider is also debatable.

The motion to reconsider must be made by a member who is on the prevailing side of the previous vote. If the vote being reconsidered was a voice vote, any member of the association who is present is considered to have been on the prevailing side and may make the motion. Once the reconsideration is adopted, the meeting is again considering the previous motion, and it must be voted on separately from the actual vote for reconsideration. When the reconsidered motion has been disposed of, it cannot be reconsidered a second time without the unanimous approval of the membership.

Reconsideration is in order and available for use at any time during the meeting at which the main motion was voted upon. The most common use for the motion is to revisit an issue previously adopted for purposes of clarifying or modifying when the original motion was incomplete or incorrect. On some occasions, the purpose of the motion will be to reverse the substance of the original motion by changing it significantly or defeating it outright.

Because reconsideration of a motion may be made only once, caution must be used by both the maker of the motion and the presiding officer to ensure that the meeting does not foreclose its consideration of an issue by prematurely disposing of a motion to reconsider. Once it has been voted upon, both the motion to reconsider and the main motion cannot be brought up again during the meeting.

4.7   **Priority of Motions.** While only one main motion may properly be considered by the association meeting at one time, subsidiary, incidental and privileged motions may be made during the consideration of a main motion. These motions may be made to modify the main motion or to modify how the meeting will consider the main motion. *Robert's Rules of Order* lists over 44 different motions and variations of motions, and each has its priority in relation to the others. A motion having higher dignity than the one currently before the meeting can be made and must be disposed of before continuing with the regular meeting business.

A motion of lesser dignity than the one being considered by the meeting cannot be made and is out of order until the higher ranking motion is disposed of by the membership. The following commonly used motions are listed in their priority ranking with the motion of highest dignity listed first:

1.   Adjourn at a fixed time.
2.   Adjourn.
3.   Recess.
4.   Reconsideration.
5.   Questions of privilege.
6.   Call for orders of the day.
7.   Lay on the table.
8.   Previous question.
9.   Limit debate.
10.   Postpone to a certain time.
11.   Amend the motion.
12.   Postpone indefinitely.
13.   Main motion.

By disposing of motions in their proper priority, the business of the meeting can be completed as intended under the rules of procedure and without confusion. It is particularly important for the presiding officer to understand the basic priority of motions in order to maintain the proper order of business during the meeting.

4.8   **Matters Out of Order.** The rules of parliamentary procedure establish an order for business of the meeting and the manner in which business is presented and disposed of by those in attendance at the meeting. A matter can be out of order when it is presented at the wrong time or when it is presented in the wrong way. Under either of these circumstances, it is the prerogative and duty of the presiding officer to rule the matter out of order.

A main motion is out of order when another main motion is already pending or when the main motion is on a subject which should arise under a different order of business on the agenda. A motion will also be out of order when a motion of higher dignity is already being considered by the meeting. An association member may be out of order if not properly recognized by the chairman or if the member seeks to make a dilatory or frivolous motion.

To call a point of order, or to demand that the proper order of business be followed, is a privileged matter, or motion, for any member. When claiming a point of order, it is proper for the member to rise and state the point. It does not require a second to be considered by the chairman. A question, or point of order, cannot be amended by another member of the association and must be decided by the presiding officer without debate.

The presiding officer may seek consultation with the association's legal advisor or parliamentarian before ruling on the point of order, but it is the presiding officer's duty to enforce the rules and the order of business of the meeting without debate or unnecessary delay. It is the right of every member who notices a departure from the rules or from the order of business to insist upon proper enforcement.

4.9   **Waiving the Rules.** It is permissible to depart from the normal order of meeting business or to return to a previous point of the meeting agenda if a motion to waive the rules of parliamentary procedure is adopted first. When a motion to waive the rules is adopted, the subject matter may be brought before the meeting out of the regular order of business, and it is not subject to a point of order by a member of the meeting. A motion to waive the rules is an incidental motion, and it must be decided by the meeting without debate. It requires a favorable vote of two-thirds of the voting interests present at the meeting for adoption, and the motion itself cannot be amended.

Waiver of the rules is an extraordinary procedure, but it has its proper place and uses in the parliamentary rules. Excessive use of the motion can be avoided when the agenda for the meeting is clear and detailed and when the presiding officer of the meeting is deliberate and well-prepared. When it does become necessary to waive the rules, the motion should be clearly stated, and the part, or parts, of the rules being waived should be specifically identified. Since the motion is not debatable and because it requires an extraordinary vote for adoption, it must be carefully and completely presented to the membership before the question is put to a vote.

4.10 **Debate.** Debate begins after a motion has been made, seconded and stated by the presiding officer to the membership meeting. Each individual desiring to debate a motion must first be recognized by the chairman of the meeting. If *Robert's Rules of Order* are being used, no member may speak more than a total of ten minutes on any single issue. A member is not permitted to speak a second time on the issue until all persons desiring to be heard the first time have had an opportunity to speak.

Members' debate must be confined to the specific issue before the meeting. Debate must be presented in a respectful manner so as to avoid personalities and personal attacks. The maker of the motion, or the person presenting the subject, is the member allowed to speak last unless a motion for the previous question is adopted to close or eliminate all debate. Any motion to limit or to close debate must be adopted by two-thirds of the voting interests present. No debate is permitted after the vote to close debate has been adopted. No debate on a motion is in order after the vote has been taken and announced by the presiding officer. During debate it is permissible for a member to ask questions when another person is debating the issue, but all questions must be asked through the chairman. If the speaker is willing to yield to the question, then the member desiring to ask the question may do so.

All main motions are debatable, as are motions to postpone a matter indefinitely and motions to rescind an action or to ratify an action. A motion to reconsider is debatable if the motion which is being reconsidered was debatable at the time it was made. Motions and matters of privilege, motions to waive the rules, motions to adjourn and to recess and certain other incidental and subsidiary motions are not debatable. When debate is permitted, the chairman of the meeting should alternate speakers between the opposing sides of the issue. The chairman may not debate for or against any issue that comes before the meeting.

4.11 **Decorum.** Decorum for a successful meeting is built on mutual respect between the membership and the presiding officer of the meeting. All issues and requests to speak should be presented through the chairman of the meeting. Members wishing to obtain the floor for any purpose should do so properly and seek the recognition of the presiding officer. Once a member assumes the floor, the rules of debate should be obeyed, and all comments should be confined to the question before the meeting. Comments and statements relating to personal motives and to personalities should not be made and may be ruled out of order by the presiding officer.

Proper decorum at a meeting is no more than the exercise of common courtesy and maintenance of respect for the rights of others. To ensure that decorum is maintained, the presiding officer of the meeting should guide members through the proper order of business. The presiding officer must require that the rules be followed at all times. At the same time, the chairman must be both flexible and patient with members who are unfamiliar with the formal rules of parliamentary procedure. The chairman should not permit conduct which is disruptive, tedious or dilatory.

CHAPTER 5

VOTING AND DETERMINATION
OF THE COLLECTIVE WILL

5.1   General.

5.2   General Consent Voting.

5.3   Voice Votes.

5.4   Voting by Show of Hands.

5.5   Roll Call.

5.6   Ballots.

5.7   Ballot Preparation.

5.8   Voting and The Presiding Officer.

5.9   Determining the Results.

5.10   Recount and Reconsideration.

VOTING AND DETERMINATION
OF THE COLLECTIVE WILL

Chapter Five

5.1   **General.**   The process of voting is the method of expressing the collective will of the membership.   There are five basic ways for that voting process to take place: (1) by "general consent," (2) by "voice vote," (3) by "show of hands," (4) by "roll call," and (5) by "ballot".   Each type of voting has its appropriate place at a membership meeting, and each type can be used effectively at a well-run meeting of the members.   Use of an inappropriate voting method, on the other hand, can result in disruption or in an actual breakdown of the meeting.

In most cases, an issue before the meeting can be decided by a majority of the votes cast.   When there is a tie vote, the motion is not carried, and the issue is lost.   Under some circumstances, the rules of parliamentary procedure require a two-thirds vote by those present and voting to adopt a motion.   On other issues, the governing documents of the community will require an extraordinary vote of the full membership, whether present or not, to adopt the issue.   Selecting the proper method of voting is essential to a successful determination of the membership's mandate or opinion.

5.2   **General Consent Voting.**   Voting by "general consent" is most often used when there is no objection to an issue before the membership.   The chairman of the meeting will simply ask if there is any objection to the motion on the floor, and, if there is none, the chairman will declare that the motion is unanimously approved by the members present.   If any member present objects to the adoption of the issue or motion before the meeting, the objection should be clearly stated when the presiding officer asks for objections.   When an objection is made, the general consent is not obtained, and the chairman of the meeting must take the vote by one of the other available methods.

5.3   **Voice Votes.** "Voice voting" is used when an issue before the meeting is relatively non-controversial. The chairman of the meeting will ask for those in favor of the issue to say "aye" and for those who are opposed to the motion to say "no." The chairman will then rule on which group carried the motion. A voice vote should be taken only when the motion requires a majority vote, and, if a member disagrees with the ruling of the chairman on the voice vote, the member may request a count by one of the other voting methods.

When voting interests are not equal or when large numbers of proxies are represented at a particular meeting, the chairman should be cautious when relying on a voice vote to determine results. The paper proxies are silent when the voice vote is called for, but they have the mandatory right to participate in the decisions of the meeting. When there is doubt about the results of a voice vote, the presiding officer should not hesitate to use another and more specific voting method.

5.4   **Voting by Show of Hands.** Voting by "show of hands" is often a simple sight verification of a voice vote and does not necessarily require that an actual count of hands be made. An exact count of the hands can be made, but, if an exact count is desired, voting by either roll call or by ballot is a more correct method. When a "show of hands" is called for by the chairman, he may request that a particular hand be raised, or he may request that each individual favoring the proposition rise from their seat and stand. As with a voice vote, the show of hands method can be misleading and inaccurate if a large number of proxies are present at the meeting or if there are weighted votes within the association membership.

5.5   **Roll Call.** A "roll call" vote requires that the name of each member present be called, allowing for a response of "yes" or "no" to be made on the issue. When a member is present by proxy, the proxy holder should rise when the member's name is called and state that he or she is representing the absent member by proxy and cast the vote for the absent member in the manner that the proxy allows.

Any member may change the vote cast at any time during the roll call prior to the announcement of the results. Once the results of

CHAPTER 6

**THE BOARD OF DIRECTORS
OF THE HOMEOWNERS ASSOCIATION**

THE BOARD OF DIRECTORS
OF THE HOMEOWNERS ASSOCIATION

Chapter Six

6.1 **General.** The homeowners association has the responsibility for the association's property and the management and operation of the community in accordance with the standards established by the governing documents. To the extent that the corporation has such authority and control, it is the board of directors that carriers out these duties and responsibilities. The term "board of directors" is synonymous with other similar terms such as "board of governors" or "board of administration," and the terms can be used interchangeably unless the bylaws of the association clearly state otherwise.

Members of the board of directors in a not-for-profit homeowners association serve without compensation unless the bylaws of the association provide to the contrary. The board's authority is comprehensive, however, and includes all of the powers and duties enumerated in general corporate law as long as the powers are not inconsistent with the provisions of the documents governing the community.

6.2 **Transition from Developer Control.** The developer or builder creates the association and appoints the first complete board of directors at the time that the homeowners association is created. The developer-controlled board maintains and operates the association until the community matures and control of the board of directors passes to the property owners. As the developer sells the individual lots, units or parcels of property, the owners become entitled to a voice on the board of directors.

If the articles of incorporation or the bylaws of the homeowners association do not specify a specific time or formula for transition, the members will be entitled to elect the individuals who will control the board when the lot or parcel owners become a majority of the association membership. In most circumstances, however, either the community documents or the law governing the specific type of owners association will establish a formula for transition.

When the time comes for transition, the developer or builder must transfer, and the new owners must accept, control of the board of directors together with all of the property and records of the association. The builder or developer does not relinquish the responsibility as developer at the time of transition. The responsibilities for warranty defects and other obligations remain with the developer even when control of the board of directors is relinquished to the new owners.

The board of directors is the legal entity representing all of the owners, and, by assuming control of the board, the owners can pursue claims against the developer in an organized and efficient manner. It is a common mistake for new owners to refuse control of their own association because they feel claims against the developer remain. In reality, their claims are best made through a board of directors controlled by the residents.

6.3   **Election and Selection.** In most circumstances, the bylaws of the homeowners association will provide the manner for the selection and the election of the members of the board of directors. Generally, there are two methods for selecting members of the board. The first, and most common, is election to the board by members of the homeowners association at an annual or special meeting. The second method of selection is by appointment to the board of directors. The appointment may be made by the developer if the developer is still entitled to representation, or it may be by the remaining members of the board of directors when a vacancy on the board occurs between meetings of the membership.

When members of the board are to be selected by election, the election is preceded by the nomination of candidates. Nominations should be allowed from the floor of the membership meeting prior to voting even when a nominating committee submits its recommendations. Balloting from the membership continues until a majority of the voting interests selects the board members who will serve in each of the vacancies to be filled.

When a vacancy arises on the board between meetings of the membership, the remaining board members may select a new member by appointment unless the bylaws of the homeowners association provide otherwise. Vacancies on the board of directors may be filled by the remaining members even if the remaining members are less than a majority of the full board. The member appointed to fill a vacancy is permitted to serve for the balance of the unexpired term of his or her predecessor unless the bylaws of the association require otherwise.

6.4   **Eligibility.** The bylaws of the homeowners association will specify and provide the eligibility requirements for the members of the board of directors. General corporate law does not require individual board members to be members of the homeowners association to be eligible for election to the board, but most association bylaws do impose a membership requirement for eligibility. While bylaws may prohibit non-members from serving on the board of directors, they should not prohibit a member desiring to be a candidate from being nominated from the floor of a membership meeting and seeking election to the board.

When eligibility is limited to property ownership and a lot or parcel is owned jointly, each of the owners is qualified to serve on the board even though only one of the owners may be designated to exercise the property's voting rights. When a lot or parcel is owned by a corporation or another type of artificial person, determining the eligibility for a representative of the property to serve on the board of directors presents a unique dilemma. If the bylaws permit, the designated voting representative of the corporation may be eligible for the board. If eligibility is contingent upon association membership, however, then the property may be effectively excluded from offering a candidate for the board since a corporation cannot sit as a member of the board of directors.

Membership in the association passes with ownership of a lot or parcel of property. When the property is sold, the membership in the association is also transferred to the new owner. When ownership is an eligibility requirement for service on the board, transfer of the property will terminate the eligibility of an individual to serve on the board of directors and create a vacancy on the board at the time of sale.

6.5   **Term.** Unless the association bylaws provide for a different term, all members of the board serve for a one-year period, and their terms will expire with the election of their successors at the next annual meeting. The bylaws may provide for longer terms in office but cannot permit a term for longer than four years, and at least one-fifth of all of the board members must be elected each year. Every homeowners association should consider the option of multiple year terms. Staggered multiple-year terms help ensure continuity and experience from one year to the next. In order to allow for a term of more than one year, the specific duration of the term must be enumerated in the association bylaws.

When a proposed board member is present at the election or has previously agreed to serve on the board of directors, the term of office begins immediately after the election has been completed and the results have been announced. If a member is elected to the board but is not present at the meeting and has not previously consented to serve, the term of office begins when the member has been notified of election and agrees to serve.

6.6   **Number.** The number of members on the board of directors must be fixed in the bylaws or in the articles of incorporation of the association, or these documents will state how the number will be set by the members of the homeowners association. Documents in many communities permit the members of the association to vary the number of members on the board of directors within certain limits. At the discretion of the community, this option in the documents allows the membership to select a size for the board that will maximize the representation of owners and the efficient operation of the association affairs.

It is important to remember that while the number on the board may be increased or decreased in the manner established in the bylaws, the term of a sitting member of the board of directors cannot be decreased or shortened by changing the number of board members. When members of the community are given the opportunity to set the size of the board by the community documents, the action should be by separate vote at a meeting of members. Consideration should appropriately be given to the type and number of parcels, the categories of owners, the overall size of the community and the length of board terms when selecting the number of board members that will best serve the community.

6.7   **Removal.** Under some circumstances, removal from the board of directors may be automatic as a result of changes in circumstance. For example, if eligibility for the board of directors is contingent upon membership in the association, a sale or transfer of the board member's property will terminate the rights of membership, including the right to serve on the board. Removal from the board of directors would be automatic at the time of sale.

Removal may also occur by recall, and, if the bylaws or the law governing the association allows, any member of the board of directors is subject to recall or removal at any time, with or without cause. If the recall procedures are successfully implemented, the recall becomes effective immediately upon completion of the necessary procedural steps. The board member or members being recalled can then take no further formal action on the homeowners association's behalf, and a vacancy on the board occurs.

6.8 **Fiduciary Relationship and Responsibility.** The members of the board of directors and all officers of the association have a fiduciary relationship with the members of the homeowners association. This fiduciary relationship imposes obligations of trust and confidence in favor of the corporation and its members. It requires the members of the board to act in good faith and in the best interests of the members of the association. It means that board members must exercise due care and diligence when acting for the community, and it requires them to act within the scope of their authority.

The fact that the association is a corporation not-for-profit, or that the members of the board are volunteers and unpaid, does not relieve them from the high standards of trust and responsibility that the fiduciary relationship requires. When a member accepts a position on the board of directors, he or she is presumed to have knowledge of the duties and responsibilities of a board member. Board members cannot be excused from improper action on the grounds of ignorance or inexperience, and liability of board members for negligence and mismanagement exists in favor of the homeowners association and the property owners.

Each board member must recognize the fiduciary relationship and the responsibilities that the board has to the homeowners association and each of its members. The board's duties must be performed with the care and responsibility that an ordinarily prudent person would exercise under similar circumstances, and the ultimate responsibilities cannot be delegated to a manager, a management company or other third party.

6.9 **Indemnification.** When members of the board of directors and officers of the homeowners association properly carry out their duties within the scope of responsibility assigned to them, they may be indemnified by the association and its members when claims or suits are brought against them for their actions. Indemnification provisions for officers and directors are routinely included in the articles of incorporation of the association, and, in most jurisdictions, insurance coverage is available to the association for exposure to risks from the indemnification obligation.

In fulfilling their duties and responsibilities, the officers and board members may use and rely on certain information provided by others when discharging assigned duties on the association's behalf. Information, opinions and reports from officers and employees of the association which the director believes to be reliable and competent may be relied upon, and the advice and opinions of legal counsel and other professionals may also be appropriately used.

CHAPTER 7

MEETINGS AND PROCEDURES
OF THE BOARD OF DIRECTORS

MEETINGS AND PROCEDURES
OF THE BOARD OF DIRECTORS

Chapter Seven

7.1   **General.** The forum for association decision-making is at the meetings of directors.   Actions of the board take place at meetings of the board, and a meeting of the board of directors includes any gathering of a quorum of the members for the purpose of conducting association business.   Meetings may be either a regular or special gathering, and they may be called by the chairman, the president, any two members of the board or any other persons who are authorized to do so by the bylaws of the association.

Unless the bylaws place a restriction on the location for a directors' meeting, it may be held wherever the board finds it appropriate and necessary. The place may include the offices of the association's attorney, accountant, manager or other appropriate location selected by the board of directors.

7.2   **Quorum and Absent Board Members.** A majority of the full board of directors is a quorum for the board unless a greater number is required in the association bylaws. A majority of that quorum has the authority to act for the full board on all matters unless some extraordinary majority is required by the association bylaws for a particular item of business. Members of the board who are not present at a meeting in any way may join the results of the meeting by signing the minutes to concur with actions taken by the directors present.

Under some special circumstances, an absent member may participate in a meeting of the board of directors by telephone and can be counted towards a quorum for the meeting. When an absent member of the board is permitted to attend by telephone, a telephone speaker should be used so that the discussion may be heard by all other board members and any association members who are present at the open meeting. If these requirements can be met, the absent board member participating by telephone may be counted for all purposes including the determination of a quorum and on all roll call votes taken at the meeting.

7.3   **Notice to Board Members.**   There are two types of notices to be given before a proper meeting of the board of directors is held. The first is for the individual members of the board, and the second is for the general association membership. The notice to members of the board can be made by first-class mail, by personal delivery or by telegram and must be given at least two days prior to the meeting itself. The provisions of the association's bylaws may provide for different notice requirements and for longer or shorter periods of time.

The bylaws may dispense with notice for regular meetings of the board, or they may provide for the waiver of notice by board members.   Waiver must be by written consent or by actual attendance at the meeting. Notice, or the waiver of notice, for members of the board of directors is often misunderstood or ignored. Good practice will dictate that proper notice be given for each meeting of the board or that a proper waiver of notice will be obtained. The evidence of the giving of notice or the waiver of notice should become part of the records of the association.

7.4   **Notice to Association Members.**   All board meetings of the association should be open to the members of the homeowners association. In some jurisdictions, the law requires that the meetings be open. The business conducted at meetings of the board of directors is the business of the homeowners association and its members. A system of notice should be adopted to advise members when board meetings will be held. The requirement for open meetings should extend to all committees of the board and executive councils which are carrying out a portion of the association's responsibilities.

It is generally not required that notice of board meetings be mailed or delivered to each member of the association. Posting of the notice of the meeting conspicuously on the property two days in advance of the meeting will satisfy the members' notice requirements in most bylaws. The bylaws of the association should be consulted to determine the exact notice requirements and any special requirements which must be met because of the nature of the business to come before the meeting of the directors.

7.5   Agenda and Meeting Procedures. The bylaws of most homeowners associations establish a set agenda for the board of directors or adopt the latest edition of *Robert's Rules of Order* as the rules of procedure that will govern board meetings. If no agenda is provided for in the bylaws, and if no rules have been adopted by the board for an agenda, *Robert's Rules of Order* lists the following agenda:

1. Reading of minutes of previous meeting.
2. Reports of standing committees.
3. Reports of special committees.
4. Special business.
5. Unfinished business.
6. New business.
7. Adjournment.

Proper parliamentary rules of procedure are to be followed throughout the course of all business meetings, and proper minutes of each meeting must be kept for inclusion in the permanent records of the homeowners association.

When deciding matters before the board, each member may rely on the advice of the association attorney, certified public accountant or other professional advisor. When a member of the board of directors has a financial interest in a decision being made at a meeting, the board member involved has an affirmative obligation to disclose the financial interest to the remaining board members. Under such circumstances, the board member may additionally choose to abstain from voting on the matter in which he has an interest.

Each member of the board shall be presumed to vote "yes" on any action taken by the board of directors unless the member specifically votes "no" or abstains from voting because of a conflict of interest. A member of the board of directors should not abstain on reasons of general principle and may do so only when a conflict of interest actually exists. The nature of the conflict and the reason for abstaining must be disclosed to the remaining members of the board of directors and recorded in the minutes of the meeting.

7.6   **Written Action.** Corporate law and the bylaws of most corporations permit the board of directors to take action without a meeting if all of the board members consent to the action in writing. The written consent will have the same effect as if a unanimous vote had been taken at a meeting. If the law or bylaws governing the homeowners association require that meetings take place only after the posting of notice for the benefit of members, the board should be guided by the priorities of these provisions, and actions by written consent of the board should only be taken in emergency circumstances.

7.7   **Membership Participation.** Members of the association do not have any authority to act for the association by reason of being a member, nor do they have the right to participate at a meeting of the board of directors even though they may have the right to receive notice of the meetings. The requirement for notice and for open board meetings extends to members of the association the right to attend and to observe the business being transacted at the meeting. It does not extend the right to participate in the meeting or to object to any action being taken by the board of directors. Each member of the association has the right to inspect and copy records from the meeting after its adjournment.

While membership participation is not required at board meetings, many communities set aside a specific part of the agenda so that individual members can make presentations to the board of directors.   Maintaining a regular portion of the agenda for membership comment helps to defuse controversy and problems, and it permits the board of directors to have regular and orderly communications from members of the association.   When considering member participation, the board should also consider how it can best be handled in an orderly fashion. A specific part of the agenda for member participation is a preferable alternative to continuous member involvement throughout the full agenda of the board meeting.

7.8   **Minutes and Records.** A record of all meetings of the board of directors must be kept in written form or in a form that is capable of being converted to a written format within a reasonable period of time. The board of directors also has custody of all the official records of the homeowners association, and the board must ensure that they are properly maintained and available for inspection by the membership. The minutes of the membership meeting and meetings of the board of directors and most other records of the association should be maintained for a minimum period of seven (7) years.

The official records of the homeowners association should be maintained in the offices of the association or with the officers of the association having responsibility for custody of the records. The records must be open for inspection by any association member or the member's authorized representative at all reasonable times. The right to inspect the homeowners association records also includes the right to obtain copies, although the association may charge a reasonable fee for the reproduction.

One part of the association records that needs special attention is the roster of members. The need to maintain it and to keep it current is overlooked by many boards of directors, even though it is frequently used and required by the documents of many communities. Many documents provide for an approval of sales which, in turn, allows the board of directors to remain current with all new owners. If the roster of members has become out-dated or if there is no approval process provided for new owners, a current list of property owners may be available in the office of the local tax collector or the recording office for deeds.

CHAPTER 8

OFFICERS OF THE ASSOCIATION

OFFICERS OF THE ASSOCIATION

Chapter Eight

8.1 **General.** The homeowners association acts through its officers and agents. The board of directors makes the policies for the association, but the officers and agents carry out these policies and administrative functions for the community. Some of the officers are merely clerical or ministerial, while others carry out substantive functions based on the policies established by the board of directors. All of the officers have an affirmative obligation to act with utmost good faith towards the association and cannot deal in the funds or the property of the association to their own advantage.

Each homeowners association must have a president, secretary and treasurer and may have one or more vice presidents. Unless the bylaws otherwise prohibit additional appointments, the board of directors may also appoint other officers and outline their duties and responsibilities. Collectively, the officers will perform the duties established in the bylaws and carry out the management responsibilities of the corporation under the policies approved by the board of directors.

8.2 **Election of Officers.** The officers of the homeowners association are elected or appointed by the board of directors. They are not elected by the membership of the association unless the bylaws or other governing document of the association specifically require a membership vote for a particular office. Except in rare circumstances, the only officers that will be elected by the full membership are those individuals that are selected to serve as chairman of a membership meeting or those who are selected as inspectors of elections to tabulate the ballots at membership meetings.

The remaining officers of the homeowners association are selected by the board of directors at the time, place and in the manner set forth in the bylaws. Like all meetings of the board of directors, the meeting of the board at which the selection or election of officers is made should be open to members of the association. A majority vote of the whole board is required for election. In most circumstances, the election will take place at the annual organizational meeting of the new board of directors. When a vacancy occurs in an office of the association, the successor may be elected or appointed at any subsequent meeting of the board of directors.

8.3   **President.** The president of the homeowners association is vested with all the powers generally given to the chief executive officer of a corporation. While specific bylaw provisions may vary the president's duties, it is generally presumed that he or she will preside at all meetings of the board and the membership. The president will execute contracts, orders and other documents in the name of the association as its agent. When signing documents, the president should indicate the capacity in which he or she is signing to avoid any personal liability since the president's signature, under most circumstances, will bind the association under a doctrine of inherent powers.

The president also assumes general charge of the day-to-day administration of the association and has the authority to authorize specific actions in furtherance of the board's policies. As chief executive officer, the president serves as spokesman for the board of directors in most matters relating to general association business. Like all officers of the association, the president has an affirmative duty to carry out the responsibilities of the office in the best interests of the association. The president serves at the will of the board of directors and can be removed with or without cause at any time by majority vote of the full board.

The president cannot, without specific board approval, borrow funds in the name of the homeowners association or otherwise act beyond the scope of the authority established by the community's governing documents and board of directors. The president does have the inherent authority to appoint committees to advise him and to advise the board. The president also has the authority to appoint certain officers to assist with the duties of the office such as vote tellers, inspectors of elections, sergeants at arms, and a temporary secretary or recorder unless the bylaws otherwise make some provision for selection of these positions.

8.4   **Secretary.** The secretary of the homeowners association is responsible for keeping and maintaining a record of all meetings of the board and the membership and is the custodian for most of the official records of the association. The position of secretary is not simply a clerical position, however. In many cases, the secretary will not actually keep the minutes of the meetings but will be responsible for obtaining someone who will do so as a recorder or assistant secretary. As the custodian of the minutes and the other official records of the association, the secretary is responsible for ensuring access to those records by the members of the association and their authorized representatives.

Unless the community documents otherwise provide, the secretary will be in charge of giving all of the required notices to both the board and association members in accordance with the law and the documents of the community. As the custodian of the records, the association secretary may also be responsible for filing the annual government reports to maintain the active status of the homeowners association.

The secretary of the association is the designated custodian of the "corporate seal." While there is no required content for the seal, the board of directors must adopt a format for it, and, when executing an instrument on behalf of the association, the seal must be used. Under most circumstances, the signature of the president will bind the corporation, and the secretary, as custodian of the seal, traditionally verifies the president's authority by also signing or attesting to the president's signature and placing the corporate seal on the appropriate order, resolution or other document.

8.5   **Treasurer.** The treasurer is the custodian of the funds, securities and financial records of the homeowners association. When the association has a manager or other employee that actually handles the funds, then the treasurer's duties will include overseeing the appropriate employees to ensure that the financial records and reports are properly kept and maintained. Unless the bylaws otherwise specify, the treasurer is responsible for coordinating the development of the proposed annual budget and for preparing and giving the annual financial report on the financial status of the homeowners association.

The treasurer does not have the authority to bind the association or the board of directors in dealing with third parties unless the board has provided express authority for the treasurer to do so. As with the association's secretary, the treasurer does not have to actually perform the day-to-day record keeping functions of the homeowners association, but the treasurer will ultimately be responsible for insuring that the financial records of the association have been maintained properly in accordance with good accounting practices.

8.6   **Vice President.** The vice president of the homeowners association is vested with all of the powers which are required to perform the duties of the association president in the absence of the president. The vice president does not automatically possess inherent powers to act in the capacity of chief executive and may act for the president only when the president is actually absent or otherwise unable to act. The vice president may assume such additional duties as are defined by the board of directors.

In many communities, the vice president will be assigned specific areas of responsibility which may include the grounds and buildings, the recreational properties or other association activities. The vice president may also be designated to serve as the executive director or the employee manager for the homeowners association. Each of these duties must be specifically conveyed by the board of directors upon the vice president, and the scope of this authority and responsibility should be defined in writing and placed in the minutes or in the bylaws of the association.

8.7   **Registered Agent and Office.** The registered agent is a ministerial officer of the association, and it is an officer that is required of all corporations by statute. In addition to naming a registered agent, each corporation must also maintain a registered office for the association, although it does not need to be the same as the corporation's main place of business. The registered agent receives all formal service of legal papers on behalf of the homeowners association, including all lawsuits.

The registered agent is an important link for the corporation since many formal and important communications will be received by this association officer. When these communications or documents are received, they must be brought immediately to the attention of the board of directors. The registered agent must be aware of the responsibilities of the office, and the board of directors may desire to assign this responsibility to a member of the current board or to the association's legal counsel.

The name of the registered agent and the street address of the registered office can be changed by the board of directors at any time by simply filing written notice with the appropriate government office. The address for the registered office of the association must be a street address. A post office box is not acceptable. The new registered agent must sign the change in designation, acknowledging and accepting the responsibilities of the position.

8.8   Other Officers. Unless prohibited in the bylaws, the board of directors may appoint other officers and grant to them duties and responsibilities that the board feels are appropriate. Other officers may include an assistant secretary, additional vice presidents and other positions which will serve merely as agents to carry out specific association responsibilities. These other offices will help divide the responsibilities of the homeowners association into manageable categories, and each office can be assigned specific authority by the board of directors to carry out the assigned duties and responsibilities.

The responsibilities of supplemental association officers may include the authority to sign liens, demand letters and checks for the association. They may include the authority to manage the day-to-day maintenance responsibilities for the community or other specific activities sanctioned by the board. Custom allows third parties to rely on agents and officers of the association. A commitment made in the normal course of business by agents and officers may bind the corporation. When creating additional offices, the board should specify, in writing, the scope of authority for the office and the specific duties and responsibilities of the officer. The limits imposed upon the officer's authority should also be expressed.

8.9   Scope of Authority. The officers and agents of the homeowners association must carry out their duties within the scope of authority conferred upon the office. The relationship between an officer and the association is that of principal and agent. When the officer is acting on the homeowners association's behalf and within the scope of his or her authority, the association is bound by the acts of the officer or agent. Individual association members or members of the public at large acting in good faith may rely on the "real" or "apparent" authority of an officer to bind the homeowners association.

The "real" authority of an association officer is that which is expressly set out in the association bylaws or in a resolution of the board of directors and which is actually known to the party dealing with the officer. The "apparent" authority of an officer is grounded in the doctrine of estoppel. It arises when the homeowners association allows or causes others to believe the officer has such authority through its actions and representations. It may exist or arise from the very nature of the office itself. Through an officer's authority, real or apparent, the association makes its financial commitments, enters into contracts for service and otherwise carries on the business of the association.

8.10 Proper Performance of Duties. Officers of the homeowners association must devote enough time and effort to the performance of their duties to insure that they are reasonably and faithfully carried out on behalf of the association. Officers are presumed to know the duties and responsibilities of the office they are assuming. They must avoid action which will result in private or personal gain from their position, and they must restrict themselves to the scope of the duties assigned to them. Officers have an affirmative fiduciary responsibility to the members of the association in the same manner as the members of the board of directors. They may also be liable to the association members for breaches in trust, fraud or negligence.

When officers are properly carrying out their duties within the scope of responsibility assigned to them, they may be indemnified by the association and its members when claims or suits are brought against them for their actions. To protect the officers and the membership which they serve, the board should maintain "errors and omissions" insurance coverage on each officer and director.

8.11 Eligibility. Unless the bylaws of the association mandate otherwise, an officer of the homeowners association is not required to be a member of the association, a member of the board, a property owner or an employee of the association. Traditionally, the president, vice president, secretary and treasurer are members of both the association and the board, but this association membership is not required by law. An individual is also eligible to hold more than one office in the association at one time.

8.12 Resignation and Removal. Any officer of the homeowners association may resign at any time by delivering his or her resignation to the association. The resignation is effective when the notice is delivered by the officer unless the notice specifies a later effective date. When the resignation is effective at a later date, the vacant office may be filled before the effective date of the resignation, provided the successor does not take office until the vacancy is effective.

Officers of the association serve at the pleasure of the board of directors unless the bylaws provide for specific terms of office or conditions for removal from the office. The removal of an officer can be done with or without cause when the board feels it is in the best interest of the association. Once the vacancy occurs, the board of directors may fill the vacant office immediately. If an officer or an agent is elected by the association members, the officer cannot be removed by the board of directors and must be removed by the membership.

8.13 Compensation. The officers of the homeowners association are not entitled to compensation for their services unless the bylaws of the association specifically permit the compensation to be paid. If compensation is allowed by the bylaws, the conditions for compensation should be strictly followed. An officer should not be allowed to fix or increase his or her own salary unless expressly authorized to do so by the articles of incorporation or the bylaws of the homeowners association.

Since the property manager or other agent may be considered an officer of the association, it is important to review the bylaws and the articles of incorporation for authority to employ and compensate a manager and other individuals who serve as agents on the association's behalf. Although compensation may not be allowed to most officers, they are entitled to reimbursement for reasonable expenses incurred in the performance of their duties. The board of directors should require a specific accounting for such expenses before any reimbursement is made.

formal provisions in the community's documents or by resolution of the board. Although formal written authority is not required for the advisory committee appointments, the better practice is to do so by written resolution of the board of directors or by letter of authority by the appointing officer.

9.4   **Committee Authority.** The board of directors has the power to appoint committees and to give them authority. The authority of the board to delegate powers to committees is not unlimited, however. The authority of a committee is restricted by the limits placed upon it by the articles of incorporation, the bylaws and the resolutions adopted by the board of directors creating the committee. When a committee is created by resolution of the board, the resolution should specifically express the powers being delegated and the limits on that power. The resolution should be in writing, although the lack of a written resolution will not destroy the effectiveness of the committee under most circumstances.

Advisory committees do not have the authority to act for or to bind the association in any way. Advisory committees are limited to fact finding, information gathering and to making recommen-dations to the appointing authority. The function and tenor of advisory committees should be documented in writing, but the failure to do so does not jeopardize their creation. These committees help to ease the responsibilities of the board of directors, but they cannot take its place.

The fact that the board creates a committee and conveys to it powers and duties does not relieve the board of directors and the individual members of the board of their ultimate fiduciary responsibility. They must ensure that the operations of the association are carried out in the best interest of the property owners, and ultimately they are responsible for all of the acts of the committees which they create.

9.5   **Committee Meetings and Minutes.** All meetings of committees of the homeowners association, whether advisory or exercising substantive authority, are open to the members of the association. Although non-committee members are always entitled to attend and observe the meetings, they have no right to participate. When a committee of the board has been delegated the authority to carry out a portion of the board's duties, the committee should comply with the notice requirements established for meetings of the board of directors. This will include notice, or waiver of notice, by members of the committee and the posting of notice in advance of committee meetings for the benefit of association members.

When the committee is advisory in nature, a formal record of the proceedings does not need to be maintained. A summary of the findings of fact or the recommendations will be sufficient, and the summary will be submitted as the committee's report to the appointing authority. If the committee has substantive authority and is carrying out a portion of the responsibilities of the board, a formal record of each meeting must be kept in the same way as the board itself maintains a record of its proceedings. As a general rule, any committee exercising authority of the board should be guided by all of the same procedural requirements that govern the board.

9.6   **Committee Reports.**   A summary of a committee's findings, conclusions and recommendations may be brought to the board or the membership either orally or in written form. It is preferable that the committee's report be in writing and that it be addressed to the secretary of the association. A synopsis of an oral report should be included in the minutes of the meeting at which the report is presented.

Upon receipt of a committee report, the meeting may accept and implement the recommendations, it may modify and change the recommendations or, finally, it may simply accept them and place them in the records of the association for future action and reference.

When the report of a committee has been received at a meeting of the board of directors or of the membership, it becomes a part of the permanent association records. Like other official records of the homeowners association, committee reports are open for inspection by members or their representatives at all reasonable times, and the members may obtain copies of the reports provided that they pay for the cost of reproduction.

9.7   **Special Councils.**   Many communities have special purpose bodies which serve a unique or special function tailored to the individual community. A "council of presidents" or a "commons council" are examples of special purpose committees. These councils are established when a community has several homeowners associations and needs a coordinated scheme of management for the entire community. A special management council may balance representation among buildings or among various geographical parts of a community to ensure participation by the entire community.

Special councils may also be established for other purposes, such as providing crime watch security or fire protection for the community or establishing a communications network among the membership. A network of floor, building or block representatives establishes a loose network, or committee, where members may rarely, if ever, actually meet as a group. These special councils or committees are, in many cases, carrying out limited special functions on behalf of the board of directors, and it is appropriate to recognize these functions and duties by formal written resolution by the governing board.

9.8 **Social Clubs.** Recreation committees, bridge clubs and other types of social organizations are not normally thought of as committees, nor as a formal part of the association's structure. If these clubs are exercising authority over a specific recreational function, if they are raising and spending funds, or if they are using common facilities with the approval of the board, their acts may be considered a part of the association activities. Social clubs or recreational committees serve a valid function for the homeowners association and should not be discouraged, but they must be handled properly within the association's framework.

The fact that social clubs may take on certain powers allowing them to make limited financial commitments on behalf of the community or to perform certain functions which may make them liable for negligence or injury occurring in the course of their events necessitates that the board deal with them as part of the association structure. When a social club or committee assumes a permanent and regular presence in the community, the board should be prepared to confirm the presence in resolution form. Proper financial accountability and adequate insurance coverage for club activities are responsibilities of the association.

CHAPTER 10

BUDGET, FINANCES AND INSURANCE

BUDGET, FINANCES AND INSURANCE

Chapter Ten

10.1 **General.** Each homeowners association should have a financial plan that sets forth the proposed expenditure of funds for the maintenance of the properties under the association's control and for the management and operation of the association itself. The financial plan, or budget, is the foundation document for the association's financial operation and stability. It provides for a preview of the coming year's expenses, and it provides a benchmark by which the previous year's expenditures can be judged and evaluated.

The budget should be prepared annually by the community for a twelve-month period. Once adopted, it becomes the basis for allocating the individual assessment shares among each of the members of the homeowners association. The manner for allocating shares among the members of the association will be established by the community documents. Upon adoption of the budget, the required annual contribution of each property owner in the community is also simultaneously set.

10.2 **General Operations.** The budget of the homeowners association should provide a detailed listing of all the expenses that the community reasonably believes will be incurred during the coming fiscal year. The main categories, or components, of the budget will govern the regular and ongoing operations of the association. These operations categories will deal with the everyday, recurring expenditures of the community, and they should identify each proposed item of expense separately, from administration to management, and from taxes to insurance.

The expenses for general operations should be listed by account and classification, and they should be set out to show the total estimated monthly and annual expenditures for each classification. It is helpful to have the categories coded with a numbering system or other identifying subtitle so that actual expenditures through the course of the fiscal year can be allocated to the appropriate category or account.

10.3   Capital Expenses and Deferred Maintenance.   A separate portion of the budget should be set aside for capital expenditures and deferred maintenance. These "reserve" categories of the budget are for items of expense that do not occur on a regular basis. These accounts will provide funds for the long term needs of the homeowners association which involve major capital repairs or replacements to the homeowners association property. They may include funds for roadways and repaving or for capital repairs to the community recreation building and other types of shared facilities. The reserve categories in the budget are designed to insure that funds will be available when the repairs or replacements are needed without the necessity of a large special assessment against individual members of the homeowners association.

When preparing the reserve categories, the board of directors should attempt to establish a formula that will take into consideration the estimated useful life of the asset and the amount of money that will be required to make the repair or replacement when it is actually needed. The reserve funds that are collected in the current fiscal year can be placed in a separate interest-bearing account until the need arises for the use of the funds. The basis or formula for establishing the reserve amounts should be stated as a part of the budget as a footnote so the information will be available for review by members of the association.

10.4   Developing the Proposed Budget.   The "proposed budget" is the preliminary draft of the homeowners association's financial plan, and it is offered by the board or other association officer for formal adoption as the budget. The development of the proposed budget may be by the association's treasurer, a financial committee, the community's management company or by the board of directors itself.

The board should bring as much expertise as possible to the development of the proposed budget. The preparation of account classifications for the proposed budget will be based on the association's financial history and the experience of the previous year's expenditures. New anticipated expenses can be estimated from comparisons in the marketplace or from the experience of other homeowners associations. Each classification should be based upon realistic estimates and should be set forth in sufficient detail so that each category can be understood and evaluated by the members of the association and by the board of directors.

10.5 **Notice and Adoption of the Budget.** The documents governing the homeowners association will establish whether the budget is to be adopted by the membership or by a vote of the board of directors. In either case, notice should be given or mailed to each member of the association before the meeting is actually held. If the budget is to be adopted by the full membership, this will allow an opportunity for them to evaluate and understand the financial plan for the coming year and to vote intelligently on its adoption. If the budget is to be adopted by the board of directors, the notice should state the time and place for the board meeting, and it should invite the individual owners to attend and observe.

At the budget meeting of the board or the membership, the budget may be amended prior to its adoption by appropriate motion and vote. A quorum of either meeting is sufficient to consider the budget, and a majority vote of the quorum is required to adopt the budget. Once the budget has been adopted, it may not be amended at a later time unless the same procedures are used for adoption of the budget amendments.

10.6 **Annual Financial Report and Financial Filings.** Each year the board of directors should provide, by mail or personal delivery to all members, a complete financial report of the actual receipts and expenditures for the previous twelve-month period. The report should show the amount of receipts by account classification, including a summary of all transactions which occurred in the reserve accounts of the homeowners association.

To the extent possible, the board of directors should plan to distribute the annual financial report as closely as possible to the distribution of the proposed budget for the coming fiscal year. This allows the membership of the homeowners association to make a comparison between the expenditures for the preceding twelve-month period and those expenditures which are being proposed for the coming twelve-month period.

Finally, each homeowners association, whether organized for profit or not-for-profit, is required to file an annual income tax return with the Internal Revenue Service. A corporation organized not-for-profit is neither tax exempt nor exempt from filing an annual tax return. The Internal Revenue Service Code allows homeowners associations special treatment in some circumstances for some of their activities including the retention of reserve funds. A proper accounting for these reserve monies is important, and the filing of an annual income tax return is a requirement for each association, and it should not be overlooked by the board of directors.

10.7 **Funding the Budget.** To fund the homeowners association's budget, the board of directors, in almost all circumstances, is granted authority to assess individual property owners for their share of the community's funding requirements. The recorded declaration of covenants and the bylaws of the association must be consulted to determine the basis for the assessment allocation. In the unlikely event that no specific allocation is made in the community's documents, then the responsibility for funding the budget should be spread equally among the parcels of property represented in the homeowners association.

The total required revenue for the fiscal year of the association is set once the budget is adopted. Before allocating the assessment shares among the members of the association, the board should first deduct the sums which will be generated from other revenue, such as interest and rental and use fees for the common property. The board of directors may also elect to reduce the total funding requirements by an amount equal to the surplus which remains from the previous year's budget.

When the amount of the annual assessments has been determined for each member, the board of directors is then required to establish a payment schedule for the owners. In many cases, the payment schedule will be set in the bylaws or in the covenants governing the association. If a schedule is set by the community documents, the board must, by resolution, determine whether it will be divided into monthly or quarterly installments. The board of directors should require that payments be made in advance so that funds are available to meet the current needs of the association as they arise.

10.8 **Time for Payment and Delinquency.** The timely remittance of assessments and assessment installments from each member is essential to the smooth functioning of the homeowners association and the proper maintenance of the community's property. The association, through its board of directors, has the power to establish and collect the assessments and to additionally establish the time when each assessment or assessment installment is due.

When exercising its authority to set the assessment levels, the board of directors must also establish specific due dates for the assessment or the assessment installments. In addition to a due date, the board should also identify the point in time when the payment becomes delinquent. The payment procedures should be contained in a resolution or in the minutes of the board of directors' meeting. They should also be included in the assessment notices which are provided to each member of the association. The clarity of the board of directors' actions and the responsibility of each member of the association is an essential ingredient to ensure timely payment by responsible members and to ensure effective enforcement against delinquent members.

10.9 **Enforcement.** The enforcement rights which the homeowners association has against delinquent members will vary depending upon the provisions of the community's documents. In the most limited circumstances, no special remedies will be provided, and the board of directors will have to pursue the obligation through normal court proceedings for a money judgment. Some community documents provide for fines or the loss of voting rights while the delinquency exists, while others will grant the association the right to place a lien on the property of the delinquent owner.

When lien rights are provided to the homeowners association, the board of directors should evidence its claim by filing a formal "claim of lien" with the appropriate recording officer in the county where the property is located. The claim of lien will become effective on the date of its recording until the money is paid by the property owner, and it will secure the unpaid amounts and the costs of collection.

The claim of lien should state the legal description for the property, the name of the property owner and the amount and date when the assessment or assessment installment became due. The claim of lien should be signed by an officer or agent of the homeowners association. Once it has been recorded, a registered or certified letter should be delivered to the delinquent property owner with a copy of the lien and a statement of the principle, interest and costs which the lien secures.

The board of directors should not be reluctant to use the collection sanctions which the community documents allow. When an owner is delinquent in his or her financial obligation to the homeowners association, the remaining association members assume an unfair share of the community's financial responsibilities. Proper enforcement policies by the board of directors help ensure that every member of the community will meet their appropriate financial obligation.

10.10 **Association Casualty Insurance.** For many homeowners associations, one of the more significant financial responsibilities is to provide adequate insurance coverage for the association and the common property. Adequate insurance coverage will include sufficient fire and casualty insurance to provide for the repair or replacement of community property in the event of a fire or other accident. The association fire and casualty policy will cover all of the common property of the association.

There are two types of casualty insurance coverage for homeowners associations to consider: (1) "named-peril," and (2) "all-risk". The "named-peril" insurance policy covers all risks specified in the policy, such as fire, theft or explosion. Occurrences not specified in the policy are not covered. An "all-risk" policy covers anything not specifically excluded by the insurance policy. If something which causes damage is not foreseen by the association or the insurance company, it is covered by the all-risk policy.

The individual property owner's insurance policy protects the owner's individual property from similar unexpected casualties. Additionally, it provides liability coverage in case someone is injured as a result of the property owner's negligence. The owner's policy may also cover living expenses incurred if the home is unusable due to the damage covered in the policy. In a condominium or cooperative, the policy also covers losses not provided for by the association's insurance.

10.11 **Association Liability Insurance Coverage.** Liability coverage is designed to protect the homeowners association and the membership from claims for personal injuries occurring on the common properties. The association insurance policy should provide for liability coverage for such occurrences.

Some of the more important exclusions from a standard liability insurance policy include the following:

(1) liability assumed under contracts;
(2) liability for automobiles, boats and aircrafts;
(3) liability for dispensing alcoholic beverages;
(4) liability for injuries to employees;
(5) liability for damages to property in the custody of the association; and
(6) liability for demolition activities.

When an association has circumstances which bring these types of risk into the community's insurance picture, consideration may be given to obtaining separate coverage for these categories of risk.

When the community is located in a flood zone, adequate flood insurance will also become a consideration for the board of directors. Insurance coverage for flood damage is available to the homeowners association but only through the Federal Insurance Administration's program. To qualify for flood insurance coverage, a community must apply and be accepted into the program by the Federal Government. If a community is enrolled in the program, individual property owners can obtain the insurance through their own insurance agents.

10.12 **Liability Insurance and Fidelity Bonding for Officers and Directors.** Liability insurance for officers and directors protects these representatives of the homeowners association from personal liability for their actions on behalf of the community. This insurance also protects the association since officers and directors, properly carrying out their duties within the scope of the responsibilities assigned to them, may be indemnified by the association and its members when claims or lawsuits are brought against them for their actions.

In some homeowners associations it is required, either by law or by the governing documents, that all persons who control and disperse funds of the association be bonded. The association will bear the cost of the fidelity bond in such circumstances as a common expense unless it is provided by a contract between the association and an independent management company.

10.13 **Workers' Compensation Insurance.** If the homeowners association employs any person to perform work for the community or the association, the association is required to provide workers' compensation insurance coverage for the employee. Workers' compensation insurance provides compensation for liability of an employee which results from an employment-related injury. The workers' compensation law in most states provides for a specific schedule of compensation in the event of a death or injury to an association employee. If the homeowners association fails to maintain the proper workers' compensation insurance coverage, the association becomes liable for the death or injury of its employee.

CHAPTER 11

AMENDING AND ENFORCING THE DOCUMENTS

AMENDING AND ENFORCING
THE DOCUMENTS

Chapter Eleven

11.1 Amending the Homeowners Association Documents. When considering amendments to the homeowners association documents, the documents themselves must be referred to for the authority to make changes and amendments. The community documents when recorded create contract rights for each owner, and the rights can only be modified as the documents allow. If the declaration of covenants or other instruments do not provide for amendment procedures, changes cannot be made unless the amendments are unanimously approved by the entire association membership.

When the documents allow a specific membership vote for an amendment, the procedures and required extraordinary majority must be obtained for the amendment to pass. The recorded community documents cannot be amended or altered by action or rule of the board of directors when membership approval is required for amendment. When the documents permit rules and regulations to be adopted and amended by the board, the rules may clarify or supplement the recorded restrictions, but they cannot change or amend them.

11.2 Proposing Amendments to the Documents. Amendments to the homeowners association documents can be made only after they have been proposed to the membership under the specific procedures provided for in the documents. If the association is regulated by a particular state law such as a condominium or cooperative statute, the amendment procedures required by the law must also be followed.

Prudent management and good practice dictate that amendments to the governing documents should not be presented to members by a simple reference to title or number of the section being amended. All proposed amendments should contain the full text of the amendment offered to the membership for consideration. A good format for an amendment to an existing section of the documents contains the full text of the provision being amended with new words inserted in the text and underlined. Words and phrases being eliminated from the existing text of a document are shown but lined through with hyphens to show that they are being deleted.

If the proposed amendment or change to the association documents is so extensive that these procedures would be confusing, an alternative format may be used. Such an alternative can set out the proposed amendment in full with a notation inserted immediately prior to the amendment in the following form: "Substantial rewording of section. See section _____ for present text." If a completely new section is being added by the amendment, the same procedure can be followed, but the notation inserted should state: "New section. Amendment does not change present text."

11.3 Adopting and Recording Document Amendments. Generally, amendments must be adopted by an extraordinary vote of the entire homeowners association membership. The required extraordinary vote will be set out in the document being amended, and the requirement may vary depending on the type of community. After the amendment has been adopted by the appropriate vote, the text of the amendment will be appropriately recorded or filed with the same official where original documents are filed or recorded.

The completed amendment should identify the name of the community or homeowners association, the official record where the original documents were recorded and the date that the amendment was adopted. The amendment should be appropriately signed by the officers of the association attesting to the validity and authority for the amendment's adoption. When the amendment process is complete, copies of the document changes should be furnished to each of the members of the homeowners association.

11.4 Amendments to the Articles of Incorporation. The procedures for proposing and adopting amendments to the articles of incorporation of a homeowners association are, in all respects, similar to those for amending other parts of the community documents. One additional step is required in most states to complete the amendment process, however. When required by a state's corporate law, upon adoption, the amendments to the articles of incorporation must be set out in articles of amendment and additionally filed with the state agency with which the corporation is registered.

11.5 Modification to the Common Property and Common Expense Responsibilities of Owners. Material modifications and alterations to the shared or common property of the homeowners association require specific approval of the owners in almost all circumstances. The required approval will be 100% of all the property owners unless the declaration of covenants or the homeowners association documents provide for another method of making material modifications or alterations.

Any amendment to the community documents attempting to change the percentage or share by which an association member shares in the common expenses will also require the approval of each owner and may also require approval by all owners of liens on property in the community.

11.6 Preserving the Residential Community Concept. The governing documents of the homeowners association set the standards for the residential character of the community and control the composition and conduct of its residents. Effective enforcement of the documents preserves the planned residential concept and the long-term community goals and standards. Enforcement procedures may also take away some rights and limit individual freedoms of residents. A delicate balance exists between enforcement procedures that protect the overall integrity of the common scheme and those which unreasonably restrict individual freedoms of the members of the homeowners association.

The principals of planned community living require that the rights of individuals must yield, in some degree, to the ownership goals of the majority. Enforceability of the documents is dependent, in large measure, on the level of approval granted in the original documents or given by the members of the association to the board of directors. Enforceability is also conditioned on the reasonableness, uniformity and consistency exercised by the board in its enforcement efforts.

11.7 Violation and Uniform Enforcement. When a violation of the governing documents of the homeowners association occurs, the desired result is always voluntary correction of the violation by the errant member. The first step in accomplishing this goal is giving notice of the violation to the member. Notice is given by the board of directors and should state the specific violation and the deadline for compliance, and should provide an opportunity for the non-conforming member to correct the problem. Standard notice procedures should be established and followed for each violation.

Uniform treatment of association residents is essential to successful enforcement. It is not permissible to create different classes of members for selective or arbitrary treatment, whether it is between renters and owners or between different classes of owners.

Knowledge of the violation and inaction by the board of directors may prejudice the association's ability to enforce a rule or covenant under the legal principle of equitable estoppel. Equitable estoppel is a basic concept of fairness that results in the forfeiture of the enforcement rights when they are not used in a uniform and timely fashion. Once knowledge of a violation is obtained, enforcement procedures must be implemented by the board of directors without unreasonable delay.

11.8 Authority to Exercise Architectural Control. Many homeowners association documents restrict the types of structures or improvements permitted on property in the development and require the prior approval of the board of directors before they are made. Such restrictions have been recognized as enforceable as long as they are for a lawful purpose and the restrictions are reasonably and clearly expressed in the governing documents. Generally, the purposes for such restrictions are to preserve the architectural integrity in the community and to maintain uniform design and style for improvements made by owners who reside in the community.

When the association documents permit the board of directors to exercise architectural control over improvements and alterations, the approval of the board cannot be arbitrarily withheld. Particular attention needs to be given to satellite dish installations. Restrictions on such dishes are common in many community documents, but the Telecommunications Act of 1996 has impacted their enforceability significantly. Under the Act, a member of the community may not be denied the right to install a satellite dish which is designed to receive video programming services and which is less than one meter in diameter. Some restrictions on the placement of a dish may be permitted, however, provided that they do not unreasonably delay or increase the cost of installation.

To ensure consistency in permitted alterations, the board should maintain a set of policy standards to judge the request of any owner wishing to make changes or additions. By maintaining a set of clear standards, it will help to ensure that requests are judged objectively and approvals or denials are not arbitrary. Ultimately under such procedures, the uniform standards and the architectural continuity can be maintained.

11.9 Fines and Penalties. The law governing corporations not-for-profit in most states authorizes a corporation to fine or penalize its members when the authority to do so is provided in the articles of incorporation or bylaws. In addition to monetary fines, the penalties may include the suspension of voting rights or the denial of membership privileges including the use of the common property.

If fines or other penalties are used as a part of the homeowners association enforcement policies, the specific amounts of fines and the specific conditions of other penalties should be clearly documented. Concise procedures for notice and for proper hearings should be established by the board of directors. It is good policy to have the assistance of the community's legal counsel when the board is using its authority to levy fines or impose penalties.

The board of directors must pay special attention if the type of housing is regulated by a special law such as a condominium or cooperative act. Many state laws place limited authority on the board of directors to impose fines and prohibit altogether the right to impose other penalties on members which would otherwise be allowed under the general corporate law.

11.10 Formal Judicial Action. The governing documents and restrictive covenants in the residential community create contract rights. These rights are enforceable in the appropriate courts. If the governing documents provide that the prevailing party is entitled to recover attorney's fees and costs in an enforcement proceeding, then the judge may award these expenses at the conclusion of a successful enforcement proceeding.

The board of directors must be sensitive to its enforcement responsibilities and the prerequisites to correct and successful enforcement. Timeliness and uniform enforcement policies are essential, and, should the need for formal enforcement arise, these standards must be met or the enforcement efforts will not be successful. The association's legal advisor should be consulted in all cases where formal enforcement procedures are being considered.

CHAPTER 12

RIGHTS AND RESPONSIBILITIES OF INDIVIDUAL OWNERS

12.1   General.

12.2   Use of the Common Area.

12.3   Guests and Tenants of a Parcel Owner.

12.4   Membership and Voting Rights in the Association.

12.5   Participation in Association Affairs.

12.6   Access to Association Records.

12.7   Financial Obligations.

12.8   Sale and Transfer of the Parcel.

RIGHTS AND RESPONSIBILITIES
OF INDIVIDUAL OWNERS

Chapter Twelve

12.1 **General.** The declaration of covenants and the other governing documents of the community are for the collective benefit of the members of the homeowners association. They establish the tenor for the community, and they define the rights and responsibilities of the individual association members. The principles of law governing homeowners associations are intended to support the community concept established by the governing documents while protecting the rights of the individual parcel owners.

Each parcel owner is presumed to have knowledge of the community's governing documents, and occupancy of the property in the community by a parcel owner must be consistent with the community concept. Under the law and the declaration of covenants, the owner of a parcel enjoys numerous rights and benefits. They may vary significantly based upon the language of an individual community's documents, but each owner is entitled to rely upon the content of the governing documents and the benefits conferred in them concerning the use of property in the community. These rights and benefits are appurtenances to the ownership of a parcel and run with the land.

12.2 **Use of the Common Area.** The right to use the easements, common areas and recreational amenities in accordance with the purposes for which they are intended is an appurtenance guaranteed to each parcel owner. The rights of parcel owners and their visitors and guests to use the common areas, however, may not hinder, nor unreasonably encroach upon, the lawful rights of other parcel owners. By example, speed bumps placed on a private road by a homeowners' association may substantially diminish the rights of individual owners to use the road and, therefore, constitute an improper or unreasonable restriction on the use of the common area. Similarly, a dock constructed on association-owned property for the benefit of a single parcel owner may also be deemed to violate the rights of the other owners entitled to the use and benefit of the common property.

The right of a parcel owner to use the common areas includes the right to peaceably assemble in the common facilities. Any parcel owner prevented from exercising the rights guaranteed for use of the common areas or recreational facilities may bring a civil action to enforce those rights.

The rights of a parcel owner to use common areas and facilities may be denied for a reasonable period of time, however, if the governing documents of the homeowners association authorize the suspension of these rights for violations of the community's covenants and restrictions. Rights of an owner to use the common facilities may also be suspended for delinquent assessments when the governing documents permit. The suspension of use rights to the common areas may not, however, impair the right of a parcel owner or the tenant of a parcel to have vehicular and pedestrian ingress and egress to and from the parcel, including the right to park an authorized motor vehicle.

12.3   Guests and Tenants of a Parcel Owner. The guests and tenants of a member of the association are covered by the provisions of the governing documents for the community.   As such, they enjoy the rights to use and occupy the common areas and property in the community in the manner authorized by the documents.

Guests and tenants are also required to comply with the covenants, restrictions and rules of the association governing the use of the properties in the community. The failure of a guest or tenant to comply with the community's governing documents subjects the individual to possible court action, eviction from the property and other sanctions authorized by the documents for any violation which they commit.

12.4   Membership and Voting Rights in the Association. Every parcel owner is entitled to membership in the homeowners association designated by the declaration of covenants as the managing entity for the community.   Each association member is assigned a voting interest by the governing documents as an appurtenance to membership in the homeowners association. Unless the governing documents provide otherwise, membership in the association extends to each owner of a parcel having multiple owners, and the voting rights of a member may not be suspended.

Additionally, as a member of the association, there often are related rights and privileges guaranteed to each member by governing documents. These include eligibility to be nominated to, and serve as a member of, the board of directors of the homeowners' association and the right to receive prior notice of all meetings of the board of directors and the membership. Copies of the association budget and the annual financial report should be available to all members at no charge, and the other records of the association should be available for inspection by members at reasonable times and places.

12.5 Participation in Association Affairs. No member of the homeowners association may act on behalf of the association simply by reason of being a member, but each member has the right to participate in important parts of the association's decision-making processes. All members have the right to attend and participate in all meetings of the membership and to exercise their voting interest, either in person or by proxy, on any and all decisions made at such meetings, including the selection of directors for the association. In some jurisdictions, a member of the association is also authorized by law to tape-record or videotape any meetings of the association membership, as well as meetings of the board of directors. The right to record such meetings may be subject to reasonable restrictions provided that the restrictions have been adopted in advance by the board of directors.

The rights and privileges granted by the governing documents are for the benefit of the community and each member of the community. No amendments may be made to the governing documents unless they are first presented to the members of the association for their approval in accordance with the requirements stated in the documents. If no threshold of approval is stated in the documents, then all members affected by the change must approve the amendments to the documents.

12.6 Access to Association Records. All records of a homeowners' association should be available to the association members. Upon request, it is appropriate for the association to provide a complete copy of the community's governing documents to any association member or prospective purchaser who asks for them. The association may charge for the actual costs for reproducing and furnishing the documents to those persons entitled to receive them.

All other official records of the homeowners association should be open to inspection and available for photocopying by members of the association or their authorized representatives. The homeowners association may adopt reasonable rules governing the frequency, time, location, notice and manner of records inspection and may impose fees to cover the costs of providing members copies of the official records.

12.7 Financial Obligations. The governing documents will specify the financial obligations for each parcel owner. In accordance with these obligations, each subsequent owner, regardless of how title to the property has been acquired, including purchase at a judicial sale, is liable for all assessments or amenity fees which come due while he or she is the owner. Assessments for the community's operations are levied pursuant to the annual budget or special assessment, and they are allocated among the individual members of the homeowners association in the manner described by the community's governing documents. The liability of the owner of a parcel for assessments is limited to the amounts properly assessed against the parcel by the homeowners' association.

A current account of the status of each member's financial obligation to the homeowners association should be maintained as a part of the association's official records, and it should be available for inspection upon request. Once assessed, the documents in most communities provide that the association has a lien on each parcel for any unpaid assessments and for attorney's fees and costs incurred by the association incident to the collection of the assessment or the enforcement of the lien. Failure to pay an assessment may also result in fines or suspension of the right to use the recreational amenities or common areas of the community when the governing documents permit.

12.8 Sale and Transfer of the Parcel. The covenants of a homeowners' association may not unreasonably restrict the right of a parcel owner to sell or transfer the owner's property. Covenants that attempt to unduly restrict a sale of property are considered to be an "improper restraint on alienation," and they have been deemed void by the courts. A parcel owner may not, however, use the right to sell or transfer a portion of the parcel to violate the original intent of the declaration of covenants, and efforts to do so have been rejected by the courts.

Prior to the sale of an individual parcel, the prospective purchaser should request a copy of the governing documents which describe the rights and obligations incident to ownership of a parcel in the community. The documents reveal the obligations of the assessments, which, if unpaid, may result in a lien against the parcel and any fee or rental amounts required for use of common facilities.

Purchasers of parcels governed by a homeowners' association are bound by constructive notice of the restrictive covenants that are imposed upon their property. The restrictions in the recorded covenants and the disclosure summary are clothed with a strong presumption of validity arising from the fact that each parcel owner purchases the parcel knowing of and accepting the restrictions imposed.

CHAPTER 13

STYLE AND FORMAT FOR ASSOCIATION FORMS AND DOCUMENTS

13.1   Membership Meeting Forms

13.2   Membership Meeting Sample Documents

13.3   Board of Directors Meeting Forms

13.4   Board of Directors Sample Documents

13.5   Committee Resolutions and Reports

13.6 Budget and Finance Forms

Form 13.61 Budget
Form 13.62 Annual Financial Report
Form 13.63 Claim of Lien
Form 13.64 Satisfaction of Lien

STYLE AND FORMAT FOR
ASSOCIATION FORMS AND DOCUMENTS

Chapter Thirteen

Various types of formalities accompany the operation of the homeowners association. They ensure that proper procedures are followed to protect members' rights and that member are advised of the business and finances being conducted on their behalf. Implementing these formal prerequisites for association meetings, membership voting and actions by the directors is not complicated, but it is essential to the proper and successful operation of the association.

The forms and sample documents that follow in this chapter are designed to assist and guide those who are responsible for conducting association affairs. They present the basic format for the formal documents that are used periodically by the homeowners association. When the bylaws of the association specify a different format or a variation in document content, the forms in this manual should yield to the requirements of the community's bylaws.

THE ESTATES HOMEOWNERS ASSOCIATION, INC.
A Corporation Not-for-Profit

NOTICE OF MEMBERS' MEETING

NOTICE IS HEREBY GIVEN, in accordance with the Bylaws of the Association, Inc., that the annual (or special) meeting of The Estates Homeowners Association will be held at the following date, time and place:

Date: January 15, 1998

Time: 7:00 p.m.

Place: Recreation Hall
         The Estates Homeowners Association
         100 Cypress Drive
         Cypress Springs, Florida   33444

                    THE ESTATES HOMEOWNERS
                    ASSOCIATION, INC.

                    By:_____
                         Secretary

Dated: This 20th day of December, 1997.

THE ESTATES HOMEOWNERS ASSOCIATION, INC.
A Corporation Not-for-Profit

PROOF OF NOTICE AFFIDAVIT

STATE OF FLORIDA
COUNTY OF ORANGE

The undersigned Secretary of The Estates Homeowners Association, Inc., being first duly sworn, deposes and says that notice of the annual meeting of The Estates Homeowners Association was mailed or hand-delivered to each member at the address last furnished to the Association in accordance with the requirements of the Bylaws at least fourteen days prior to the annual meeting.

Dated this 20th day of December, 1997.

_____
Secretary

The foregoing Affidavit was acknowledged before me this 20th day of December, 1997, by Nancy Thomas, the Secretary of The Estates Homeowners Association, Inc.

_____
Notary Public

My commission expires:

PROOF OF NOTICE AFFIDAVIT
FORM 13.12

THE ESTATES HOMEOWNERS ASSOCIATION, INC.
A Corporation Not-for-Profit

AGENDA
MEMBERSHIP MEETING
January 15, 1998

1.   Calling of roll and certifying of proxies.

2.   Proof of notice of meeting or waiver of notice.

3.   Reading and disposal of any unapproved minutes.

4.   Reports of officers.

5.   Reports of committees.

    a. Recreational Committee.
    b. Audit Committee.
    c. Bylaws Committee.

6.   Election of inspectors of election.

7.   Election of directors.

    a. Report of Nominating Committee.
    b. Nominations from the floor.
    c. Introduction and remarks of nominees.
    d. Adoption of resolution for number of directors.
    e. Voting.

8.   Unfinished business.

    a. Consideration of Budget Committee recommendations.
    b. Adoption of budget.

9.   New business.

    a. Consideration of amendments to bylaws.
    b. General discussion by members.

10.   Adjournment.

AGENDA FOR MEMBERS' MEETING
FORM 13.13

THE ESTATES HOMEOWNERS ASSOCIATION, INC.
A Corporation Not-for-Profit

PROXY
January 15, 1998
Membership Meeting

TO: Secretary
       The Estates Homeowners Association, Inc.
       100 Cypress Drive
       Cypress Springs, Florida 33444

       The undersigned hereby appoints the Secretary of the Association or _____, attorney and agent with the power of substitution for and in the name, place and stead of the undersigned, to vote as proxy at the membership meeting of the Association, to be held at the Recreation Hall, January 15, 1998, at 7:00 p.m, and any adjournment thereof, according to the number of votes that the undersigned would be entitled to vote if then present upon the matters set forth in the Notice of Meeting dated December 20, 1997, a copy of which has been received by the undersigned.

       (In no event shall this proxy be valid for a period longer than 90 days after the date of the first meeting for which it was given.)

DATED this _____ day of January, 1998.

                  Owner/Member

                  _____

                  _____

                  Lot Number: _____
                  (or Property Address)

GENERAL PROXY
FORM 13.14

THE ESTATES HOMEOWNERS ASSOCIATION, INC.
A Corporation Not-for-Profit

PROXY
January 15, 1998
Membership Meeting

TO: Secretary
The Estates Homeowners Association, Inc.
100 Cypress Drive
Cypress Springs, Florida 33444

The undersigned hereby appoints the Secretary of the Association or _____, attorney and agent with the power of substitution for and in the name, place and stead of the undersigned, to vote as proxy at the membership meeting of the Association, to be held at the Recreation Hall, January 15, 1998, at 7:00 p.m, and any adjournment thereof, according to the number of votes that the undersigned would be entitled to vote if then present in accordance with the specifications hereinafter made, as follows:

1.   Election of Board of Directors (vote for three).

Sara Harris   _____
William Marshall   _____
Conner Wesley   _____

_____   _____

2.   Should the amendment to the bylaws of The Estates Homeowners Association be amended to allow directors to serve for a term of two (2) years?

Yes_____   No_____

Owner/Member

Dated:_____   _____

_____
Lot Number: _____
(or Property Address)

LIMITED PROXY
FORM 13.15

THE ESTATES HOMEOWNERS ASSOCIATION, INC.
A Corporation Not-for-Profit

VOTING CERTIFICATE

TO: Secretary
The Estates Homeowners Association, Inc.
100 Cypress Lane
Cypress Springs, Florida 33444

The undersigned is the record owner of that certain lot or parcel of real property in THE ESTATES residential subdivision shown below, and hereby constitutes, appoints and designates as the voting representative for the membership interest of said undersigned pursuant to the Bylaws of The Estates Homeowners Association.

The aforenamed voting representative is hereby authorized and empowered to act in the capacity herein set forth until such time as the undersigned otherwise modifies or revokes the authority set forth in this voting certificate.

DATED this 1st day of December, 1997.

Owner/Member

_____

_____

Lot Number: _____
(or Property Address)

**VOTING CERTIFICATE
FORM 13.16**

BALLOT

1.   The following have been nominated to serve for a term of one year on the Board of Directors of The Estates Homeowners Association. There are three vacancies on the Board of Directors, and you may vote for up to three individuals by placing a check mark next to their names. A ballot voting for more than three individuals will be disallowed.

Sara Harris   _____

William Marshall   _____

Conner Wesley   _____

Carl Owen   _____

Ann Peck   _____

_____   _____

_____   _____

2.   Should the budget recommended by the Budget Committee for the next fiscal year be adopted?

Yes_____   No_____

3.   Should the Bylaws of The Estates Homeowners' Association, Inc., be amended to allow for directors to serve for a term of two (2) years in accordance with the full text of the proposed amendment which accompanied the mailing of the meeting notice?

Yes_____   No_____

BALLOT FOR BOARD ELECTION
FORM 13.17

MEMBERSHIP MEETING
PRE-MEETING CHECKLIST

1. Notice Confirmation and Date of Mailing   _____

2. Affidavit of Notice by Secretary   _____

3. Selection of Presiding Officer   _____

4. Selection of Secretary or Recorder for Meeting   _____

5. Identification of Reports to be Presented   _____

6. List of Members Making Nominations   _____

7. List of Members Making Procedural Motions   _____

8. Listing of Potential Nominees   _____

9. Selection of Vote Tellers (Inspectors of Election)   _____

10. Ballot preparation and production   _____

11. Display Board for Nominees   _____

12. Organization for Check-in Stations   _____

13. Organization for Meeting Room
    (Seating, Microphones, Podium, etc.)   _____

14. Designation of Smoking and Non-Smoking Areas   _____

15. Copy of Rules of Procedure   _____

16. Copy of Community Documents and Association
    Articles of Incorporation and Bylaws   _____

PRE-MEETING CHECKLIST
FORM 13.21

CHAIRMAN'S MEETING GUIDE

I.   CALL TO ORDER:

"The 1998 annual membership meeting of The Estates Homeowners Association, Inc., will now come to order. The first order of business is determination of a quorum."

II.   CALLING THE ROLL AND
      CERTIFYING THE PROXIES:

"The secretary will please call the roll."

or

"The number of members present in person and by proxy has been determined during the check-in procedure. There are 50 members present in person and 30 members are represented by proxy. A quorum of the association is present."

III. PROOF OF NOTICE:

"The affidavit of the secretary of the association, stating that notice has been given in accordance with the bylaws of the association, has been presented to the chairman. The proof of notice shall be filed with the permanent records and is available for inspection by the members."

IV.   READING OF MINUTES:

"The next order of business is the reading of minutes from the last meeting."

(Mr. Wesley will move to waive reading; Mr. Marshall will second.)

V.   NOMINATIONS:

"The next order of business is the nomination for the board of directors."

(Recognize Mr. Owen, chairman of the nominating committee, to give report of nominating committee.)

"The candidates recommended by the nominating committee are received as nominees. Are there further nominations from the floor?"

(Ms. Peck and Ms. Harris will have nominations.)

"Are there further nominations? If there are no further nominations, the chairman declares that the nominations are now closed."

VI.   ELECTIONS:

"Election of members to serve on the board of directors will now begin. The chairman appoints Ms. Harris, Mr. Wesley and Mr. Marshall as inspectors of election."

"Members may mark their ballots and hand them to the inspectors. Members may vote for up to 3 candidates - any ballot voting for more than 3 will be disallowed."

(The meeting will stand in informal recess until ballots are counted. Results to be announced when meeting is reconvened.)

VII.   UNFINISHED BUSINESS:

"Is there unfinished business to come before the meeting?"

(Mr. Wesley will move that budget reserves be waived.)

CHAIRMAN'S MEETING GUIDE (cont.)
FORM 13.22

VIII.   NEW BUSINESS:

"New business is now in order, and the first item to be considered is the schedule of amendments to the bylaws. Without objection, chairmanship of the meeting will be assumed by the association's attorney to handle the presentation, explanation and voting on the amendments."

(If there are no objections, the attorney will assume the chairmanship of the meeting until consideration of the amendments is complete. Ms. Harris will move adoption of the amendments; Mr. Marshall will second.)

IX.   ADJOURN:

"Is there any further business to come before the meeting?"

(If there is no further business, Mr. Wesley will move to adjourn the meeting; Mr. Marshall will second.)

SAMPLE MOTIONS

To make a motion, a member must rise and address the presiding officer of the meeting by title and state the motion that the member wishes to make. Each motion will be preceded by a preface in substantially the following form:

"Mr. Chairman, I move that..."

The motion is then stated and must be seconded before it can be considered further by the meeting.

I.   **MAIN MOTIONS**

A. Waiver of Minutes: "...the reading of the minutes from the previous meeting be waived and that the minutes be accepted as presented by the Secretary."

B. Waiver of Treasurer's Report: "...the reading of the Treasurer's Report be waived and that the report be filed with the financial records of the association for audit."

C. Adoption of Budget: "...the budget recommended by the Budget Committee be adopted for the 1998 fiscal year of the homeowners association."

D. Approval of Architectural Modifications: "...architectural modifications to the exterior of homes be allowed for installation of fences in excess of five (5) feet in accordance with the uniform standards adopted by the Board of Directors."

E. Adoption of Document Amendments: "...the schedule of amendments to the bylaws of the association be approved as presented to the membership meeting."

II.   **SUBSIDIARY MOTIONS**

A. To Amend: "...the motion to allow for material modifications to the exterior of homes be amended to allow for the enclosure of patios."

SAMPLE MOTIONS
FORM 13.23

B. Previous Question: "...the previous question now be put," or "I move the previous question." (Debate ceases and the meeting proceeds to vote - requires a two-thirds vote for adoption.)

C. Postpone to a Time Certain: "...the consideration of the alteration of the swimming pool enclosures be postponed until the annual meeting of the association in 1998."

D. Limit Debate: "...the debate be limited to three (3) minutes per person." (Requires a two-thirds vote for adoption.)

E. Postpone Indefinitely: "...consideration of the motion be indefinitely postponed."

III.   **INCIDENTAL MOTIONS**

A. Closing Nominations: "...the nominations for the Board of Directors now be closed."

B. Divide the Question: "...the main motion be divided to allow for a separate vote on the schedule of amendments to the bylaws and the schedule of amendments to the covenants and restrictions."

C. Waiver of the Rules: "...the rules be waived and the meeting return to the unfinished business portion of the agenda." (Requires a two-thirds vote for adoption.)

IV.   **PRIVILEGED AND UNCLASSIFIED MOTIONS**

A. Adjourn at a Fixed Time: "...the meeting of the membership adjourn at the hour of 10:30 p.m."

B. Adjourn and Reconvene: "...upon tabulation of the votes on the amendments to the bylaws of the association, if it is determined that the extraordinary majority necessary to adopt the amendments is not present, that the meeting be adjourned

SAMPLE MOTIONS (cont.)
FORM 13.23

until March 23, 1998, at the hour of 7:30 p.m. for purposes of obtaining the extraordinary majority. I further move that the votes present be recorded and counted at the reconvened portion of the meeting on March 23, 1998."

C. Recess: "...the meeting stand in recess until the tabulation of votes has been completed."

D. Reconsideration: "...the motion approving the architectural modifications to the exterior of individual homes be considered." (Mover must have voted on the prevailing side of the original motion.)

E. Ratify Act of Board: "...the expenditures for the repair of the storm drainage to the roof of the Recreation Hall be ratified and approved."

THE ESTATES HOMEOWNERS ASSOCIATION, INC.
A Corporation Not-for-Profit

ANNUAL MEMBERSHIP MEETING MINUTES

The meeting was called to order at 7:30 p.m., Monday, January 15, 1998, in the recreation hall by the President. The President announced that the first order of business was the calling of the roll and the certifying of the proxies. Upon its completion, it was announced that 100 units were represented in person and 50 units were represented by proxy. The President declared that a quorum of the 200 members was present.

The President next called upon the Secretary to present the affidavit for proof of notice and directed it to be annexed to the minutes of the meeting and made a permanent part of the Association's official records. The President stated that the next item of business was the reading of the minutes from the last members meeting. Upon a motion made by Mr. Wesley and seconded by Mr. Marshall, and upon discussion, it was unanimously carried by voice vote that the reading of the minutes be waived.

The next order of business was the reports of officers and committees. The President recognized the Treasurer who gave the financial report for the preceding twelve months. Upon completion of the presentation, the President directed that it be annexed to the minutes of the meeting and distributed to the membership.

Under reports of committees, the President recognized the Chairman of the Nominating Committee, Mr. Owen, who reported that the Committee had nominated the following individuals to serve on the Board of Directors for a term of one year:

Sara Harris
William Marshall
Ann Peck

MINUTES OF MEMBERSHIP MEETING
FORM 13.24

The President declared the report received and the individuals nominated for the Board of Directors. The President then asked for further nominations from the floor. The following individuals were nominated from the floor:

> Conner Wesley
> Carl Owen

The President then appointed the Association's Vice President and Mr. Campbell to serve as inspectors of election and directed that the members mark their ballots. The President then stated that, without objection, the meeting would stand in recess until the tabulation of the ballots was completed.

Upon reconvening the recessed meeting, the President called upon the Vice President to announce the results of the election. The Vice President then stated that the following individuals were elected to serve for a term of one year on the Board of Directors:

> Sara Harris
> Conner Wesley
> William Marshall

The President next asked for items of unfinished business. Mr. Anderson moved that the budget recommended by the Budget Committee for the coming fiscal year of the Association be adopted. The motion was seconded, and, at the conclusion of the discussion, the motion was unanimously passed by a voice vote. The President declared that the motion was adopted.

The President then stated that the next item on the agenda was consideration of new business. There being no new business to come before the meeting and no further members seeking recognition, upon a motion duly made, seconded and unanimously carried, the President stated that the meeting was adjourned at the hour of 8:30 p.m.

_____
Secretary

MINUTES OF MEMBERSHIP MEETING (cont.)
FORM 13.24

THE ESTATES HOMEOWNERS ASSOCIATION, INC.
A Corporation Not-for-Profit

ROSTER OF ASSOCIATION MEMBERS

Lot No.	Members and Addresses	Designated Voter
1	Sara Harris 101 Cypress Lane Cypress Springs, FL 33444 Tel. No. (111) 999-7101	Sara Harris
2	William Marshall 102 Cypress Lane Cypress Springs, FL 33444 (no telephone)	William Marshall
3	Elliot Peck Ann Peck 103 Cypress Lane Cypress Springs, FL 33444 (telephone no. unknown)	Ann Peck
4	Carl Owen Nancy H. Owen 104 Cypress Lane Cypress Springs, FL 33444 Tel. No. (111) 999-7104	Carl Owen
5	Conner Wesley Chollet Wesley 105 Cypress Lane Cypress Springs, FL 33444 Tel. No. (111) 999-7105	Conner Wesley
6	ABP Corporation 113 Main Street Cypress Springs, FL 33444 Tel. No. (111) 999-7106 Attn: David Dodd, Pres.	David Dodd

ROSTER OF ASSOCIATION MEMBERS
FORM 13.25

THE ESTATES HOMEOWNERS ASSOCIATION, INC.
A Corporation Not-for-Profit

NOTICE OF DIRECTORS' MEETING

TO: Members of the Board of Directors

1. Sara Harris
2. Ann Jones
3. David Smith
4. Conner Wesley
5. William Marshall

NOTICE IS HEREBY GIVEN that a meeting of the Board
of Directors of The Estates Homeowners Association, Inc., will be
held at the following date, time and place:

Date: January 16, 1998

Time: 9:00 a.m.

Place: Card Room
Recreation Hall
100 Cypress Lane
Cypress Springs, Florida 33444

Dated: January 10, 1998

_____
Secretary

NOTICE TO BOARD MEMBERS
FORM 13.31

THE ESTATES HOMEOWNERS ASSOCIATION, INC.
A Corporation Not-for-Profit

NOTICE TO ASSOCIATION MEMBERS OF
MEETING OF BOARD OF DIRECTORS

NOTICE IS HEREBY GIVEN that a meeting of the Board of Directors of The Estates Homeowners Association, Inc., will be held at the following date, time and place:

Date: January 16, 1998

Time: 9:00 a.m.

Place: Card Room
Recreation Hall
100 Cypress Lane
Cypress Springs, Florida 33444

The purpose of the meeting will be to consider assessments for replacing landscaping in common areas and for purposes of repainting the exterior surfaces of the Recreation Hall.

This notice has been posted upon the Recreation Hall bulletin board this 13th day of January, 1998, by order of the Board of Directors.

THE ESTATES HOMEOWNERS
ASSOCIATION, INC.

By:_____
Secretary

NOTICE TO ASSOCIATION MEMBERS
FORM 13.32

THE ESTATES HOMEOWNERS ASSOCIATION, INC.
A Corporation Not-for-Profit

WAIVER OF NOTICE OF MEETING
OF BOARD OF DIRECTORS

We, the undersigned, being all of the members of the Board of Directors hereby agree and consent to the meeting of the Board to be held on the date and time, and at the place designated hereunder, and do hereby waive all notice whatsoever of such meeting and of any adjournment, or adjournments, thereof.

We do further agree and consent that any and all lawful business may be transacted at such meeting, or at any adjournment thereof. Any business transacted at such meeting or at any adjournment, or adjournments, thereof shall be as valid and legal and of the same force and effect as if such meeting, or adjourned meeting, were held after notice.

Date: January 16, 1998

Time: 9:00 a.m.

Place: Card Room
Recreation Hall
100 Cypress Lane
Cypress Springs, Florida 33444

Dated: January 10, 1998

_____   _____
Member, Board of Directors   Member, Board of Directors

_____   _____
Member, Board of Directors   Member, Board of Directors

_____
Member, Board of Directors

WAIVER OF NOTICE BY DIRECTORS
FORM   13.33

THE ESTATES HOMEOWNERS ASSOCIATION, INC.
A Corporation Not-for-Profit

AGENDA FOR REGULAR MEETING
OF THE BOARD OF DIRECTORS

The order of business for the regular meeting of the Board of Directors shall be as follows:

1.   Reading of minutes of the previous meeting.

2.   Report of Manager.

3.   Reports of Officers.

4.   Unfinished business.

5.   New business.

6.   Comment and discussion by parcel owners on all matters to be considered by the Board.

7.   Adjournment.

**AGENDA OF BOARD MEETING
FORM 13.34**

THE ESTATES HOMEOWNERS ASSOCIATION, INC.
A Corporation Not-for-Profit

MINUTES OF MEETING OF BOARD OF DIRECTORS

The meeting of the Board of Directors was held on the date, time and at the place set forth in the notice of meeting fixing such time and place and attached to the minutes of this meeting. Notice of the meeting was posted on the bulletin board in the Recreation Hall forty-eight hours prior to the meeting.

There were present the following:

Sara Harris   David Smith

Ann Jones   Conner Wesley

William Marshall

being all the members of the Board of Directors.

After the meeting was called to order, a motion was made, seconded and unanimously adopted waiving the reading of the minutes from the previous meeting. Next, the Manager presented a report on the bids for insurance for the coming year and recommended that the lowest bid be accepted. Upon a motion duly made, seconded and unanimously carried, it was

RESOLVED, that the bid of the Florida Insurance Company, being the lowest bid, be accepted and that they be directed to provide the insurance for the association property for the next calendar year.

The President stated that there were no reports of officers and no unfinished business. The President then asked if there was any new business to come before the meeting. There being no new business, the President then recognized the member owners present for comments and discussion.

MINUTES OF BOARD MEETING
FORM 13.41

Mr. Wesley, 105 Cypress Drive, addressed the Board regarding safety in the swimming area. The President advised that the Board would review the matter in more detail. Ms. Harris, 101 Cypress Drive, next addressed the Board on the speed of vehicles passing along the main entrance road to the community. The President directed that the Manager notify the City and request that the roadway area be more closely patrolled.

There being no further business to come before the meeting and upon a motion duly made, seconded and unanimously carried, the President declared the same adjourned.

Date: _____   _____
                                   Secretary

THE ESTATES HOMEOWNERS ASSOCIATION, INC.
A Corporation Not-for-Profit

WRITTEN ACTION BY THE BOARD OF DIRECTORS

The Board of Directors of The Estates Homeowners Association, Inc., determining that an emergency exists, and, by unanimous written action, adopts the following resolutions:

1   RESOLVED, that the windstorm damage caused to the roof of the Recreation Hall be repaired immediately to prevent further damage to the interior of the building.

2.   RESOLVED, that the President of the Association be and is hereby authorized and directed to obtain three bids and to accept the lowest responsible bid for the purpose of commencing the repairs to the roof of the Recreation Hall.

3.   RESOLVED, that sufficient monies be made available from the Association budget for the purpose of paying for the repair to the Recreation Hall.

4.   RESOLVED, that a special meeting of the Board of Directors be called, after proper notice has been posted for the benefit of all the members, for the purpose of reviewing these written actions of the Board of Directors and for discussing further the wind damage to the community.

DONE by unanimous written consent this 16th day of January, 1998.

_____   _____
Member, Board of Directors   Member, Board of Directors

_____   _____
Member, Board of Directors   Member, Board of Directors

_____
Member, Board of Directors

THE ESTATES HOMEOWNERS ASSOCIATION, INC.
A Corporation Not-for-Profit

A RESOLUTION OF THE BOARD OF DIRECTORS ESTABLISHING PROCEDURES FOR THE COLLECTION OF DELINQUENT ASSESSMENTS.

BE IT HEREBY RESOLVED by The Estates Homeowners Association, Inc., as follows:

Section 1.   THAT all assessments, or assessment installments, not received by the Association by the 15th day of the month shall be deemed delinquent and the management company shall notify the lot owner of the delinquency by regular U.S. mail.   A copy of the notification shall be placed in the Association records for the unit and provided to the Association's legal counsel.

Section 2.   THAT any assessment, or assessment installment, not paid within thirty (30) days from the date when due, shall be secured by a claim of lien as provided in the community documents. The manager shall notify the legal counsel and instruct counsel to record the claim of lien, notify the delinquent owner of the recording thereof and advise such owner, by certified mail, that the assessment, together with all costs, must be paid within thirty (30) days or foreclosure proceedings will be filed to collect the delinquent monies.

Section 3.   THAT legal counsel shall be, and is hereby, authorized to commence foreclosure proceedings against any lot owner who remains delinquent after receiving the notice provided for in Section 2.

ADOPTED by the Board of Directors this 30th day of September, 1998.

THE ESTATES HOMEOWNERS
ASSOCIATION, INC.

By:_____
              Secretary

RESOLUTION OF PROCEDURE
FORM   13.43

THE ESTATES HOMEOWNERS ASSOCIATION, INC.
A Corporation Not-for-Profit

STATEMENT OF ASSOCIATION POLICY

EFFECTIVE DATE: January 10, 1997

SUBJECT: FUNCTIONS INVOLVING LARGE NUM-
BERS OF VISITORS AND GUESTS ON THE RE-
CREATION AND COMMON AREAS.

PROBLEM: Uncontrolled and unlimited use of the common
areas for functions with large numbers of guests and visitors
may interfere or infringe on the rights of other owners to use
the common property and other facilities of the Association.

STATEMENT: The operation and control of the Association's
property and the common property is the responsibility of
the Homeowners Association. All owners are entitled to the
quiet enjoyment of their home and reasonable use of the
common properties. When an owner or group of owners
holds a function with a large number of visitors and guests,
it is the desire of the Board of Directors to permit the
function and also preserve the community's security and the
rights of the non-participating owners to use the common
property   without   unnecessary   interference   and
inconvenience.

POLICY: 1. No owner shall hold an activity or function at
which more than twenty-five (25) persons will be invited
unless it shall first be approved by the Board of Directors.

2. The request to hold an activity or function shall
be in writing and state the nature of the event, the
approximate number of guests and other information
pertinent to the event.

POLICY STATEMENT
FORM 13.44

3. The consent of the Board shall not be unreasonably withheld; however, the Board may impose reasonable conditions and restrictions on the use of the property to ensure that non-participating owners are not unreasonably interfered with by the owner holding the function.

THE ESTATES HOMEOWNERS ASSOCIATION, INC.
A Corporation Not-for-Profit

A RESOLUTION OF THE BOARD OF DIRECTORS CREATING A COMMITTEE OF BOARD TO SELECT AND RECOMMEND A MANAGEMENT COMPANY FOR THE COMMON PROPERTY.

BE IT HEREBY RESOLVED by the Board of Directors of The Estates Homeowners Association, Inc., as follows:

Section 1.   THAT a committee for the selection of a management company for the common property is hereby created, and Sara Harris, William Marshall and Conner Wesley are appointed to serve as members of the committee. Sara Harris shall serve as the chairman of the committee.

Section 2.   THAT the committee is authorized to incur expenses in carrying out its duties in an amount not to exceed $100.00.

Section 3.   THAT the committee shall have the authority to investigate and interview candidate companies on behalf of the Board of Directors and shall select from the candidates the three companies which the committee feels are best qualified to provide the management services and shall recommend them, in order of preference, to the full Board of Directors prior to the next regular quarterly meeting.

Section 4.   THAT the committee shall not be authorized to retain or hire any company for the position or otherwise expend, or commit to expend, any funds of the Association except as specifically authorized by this resolution.

ADOPTED by the Board of Directors this 10th day of January, 1998.

(CORPORATE SEAL)   THE ESTATES HOMEOWNERS
                          ASSOCIATION, INC.

ATTEST:
                          By:_____
_____   President
Secretary

RESOLUTION CREATING COMMITTEE
FORM   13.51

THE ESTATES HOMEOWNERS ASSOCIATION, INC.
A Corporation Not-for-Profit

DECLARATION OF THE PRESIDENT

COMES NOW, Conner Wesley, President of The Estates Homeowners Association, Inc., and does hereby exercise the authority granted in the bylaws of the Association and does state and declare as follows:

1.   THAT, there is created a bylaw committee to study and evaluate the bylaws of the Homeowners Association.

2.   THAT, the membership for the committee shall consist of William Marshall, Sara Harris and Jacob Whitfield. Jacob Whitfield is hereby designated to serve as chairman of the committee.

3.   THAT, the committee shall make recommendations for proposed amendments to the bylaws of the Homeowners Association and shall advise the President on any amendments prior to November 15, 1998.

4.   THAT, the committee shall not have the authority to act for or to bind the Association nor shall it have the authority to expend any funds of the Association.   The existence of the committee shall terminate upon submitting its final report to the President.

DONE this 30th day of September, 1998.

THE ESTATES HOMEOWNERS
ASSOCIATION, INC.

By:_____
President

DECLARATION CREATING COMMITTEE
FORM 13.52

THE ESTATES HOMEOWNERS ASSOCIATION, INC.
A Corporation Not-for-Profit

NOMINATING COMMITTEE REPORT

TO: SECRETARY
        THE ESTATES HOMEOWNERS ASSOCIATION, INC.

FROM: 1998 NOMINATING COMMITTEE

The nominating committee appointed by the Board of Directors for the 1998 membership meeting has met and does recommend and hereby nominates the following individual to fill the unexpired term of David Smith who resigned due to ill health:

Conner Wesley

The committee further recommends and hereby nominates the following individuals for the terms expiring at the annual members' meeting in 1998:

William Marshall

Sara Harris

Susan Johnson

Respectfully submitted this 1st day of December, 1998.

NOMINATING COMMITTEE

_____
Chairman

_____
Member

_____
Member

**NOMINATING COMMITTEE REPORT
FORM 13.53**

THE ESTATES HOMEOWNERS ASSOCIATION, INC.
A Corporation Not-for-Profit

REPORT OF THE SPECIAL BYLAW COMMITTEE

TO: PRESIDENT AND MEMBERS OF THE BOARD OF
          DIRECTORS

FROM: SPECIAL BYLAW COMMITTEE, BY APPOINTMENT
          OF THE PRESIDENT, SEPTEMBER 30, 1998

The special bylaw committee met on three occasions to evaluate and to consider amendments to the Homeowners Association's bylaws. As a result of the committee's study, the following changes are recommended:

1. The Association establish a standing committee for budget and finance.

2. The Association revise its fining policy to limit the amount to no more than $50.00.

3. The Association establish a uniform procedure for identifying new owners and providing them copies of the community's documents.

4. The Association delete the section of the bylaws allowing members of the Board of Directors to abstain from voting.

5. The Association amend the section of the bylaws relating to the term of office for Board members to permit members to serve for staggered terms of two years.

Respectfully submitted this 23rd day of October, 1998.

_____
Chairman
_____
Member
_____
Member

COMMITTEE REPORT
FORM 13.54

THE ESTATES HOMEOWNERS ASSOCIATION, INC.

1998 BUDGET

I.	General Operation Expenses		Monthly	Annual
	A.	Administration & Office Expenses	$ 100.00	$ 1,200.00
	B.	Management Fee	700.00	8,400.00
	C.	Cleaning (Rec. Hall)	100.00	1,200.00
	D.	Pool Maintenance and Supplies	200.00	2,400.00
	E.	Lawn & Grounds Maintenance	500.00	6,000.00
	F.	Electricity	50.00	600.00
	G.	Property Taxes	260.00	3,120.00
	H.	Insurance	110.00	1,320.00
	I.	Miscellaneous Services		
		1) Accounting	50.00	600.00
		2) Legal	30.00	360.00
		3) Pest Control	20.00	240.00
	J.	Security	100.00	1,200.00
		Subtotal	**$ 2,220.00**	**$26,640.00**
II.	Capital Expenses & Deferred Maintenance			
	A.	Painting (Rec. Hall)	$ 384.00	$ 4,608.00
	B.	Pool Repainting	50.00	600.00
	C.	Roof Replacement (Rec. Hall)	250.00	3,000.00
	D.	Miscellaneous Reserves	30.00	360.00
		Subtotal	**$ 714.00**	**$ 8,568.00**
		TOTAL BUDGET	**$ 2,934.00**	**$35,208.00**

BUDGET
FORM 13.61

III.   **Budget Notes**

A.   Each member shall be assessed $234.72 for the year, payable $19.56 per month.

B.   Repainting of the recreation hall to occur every 8 years and one-eighth of the cost is allocated to each fiscal year.

C.   Pool repainting to occur every third year and one-third of the cost is allocated to each fiscal year.

D.   Replacement of recreation hall roof to occur every 20 years and one-twentieth of the total estimated cost is allocated to each fiscal year.

E.   Miscellaneous reserves are for items of deferred maintenance and repair which are required as a result of unexpected damage or accident and not otherwise anticipated in general operation or other reserve categories.

THE ESTATES HOMEOWNERS ASSOCIATION, INC.

ANNUAL FINANCIAL REPORT
FOR 1998 CALENDAR YEAR

I. General Operation Expenses

		Budgeted Expenses	Actual Expenses
A.	Administration & Office Expenses	$ 1,200.00	$ 1,180.00
B.	Management Fee	8,400.00	8,400.00
C.	Cleaning (Rec. Hall)	1,200.00	1,750.00
D.	Pool Maintenance and Supplies	2,400.00	2,495.00
E.	Lawn & Grounds Maintenance	6,000.00	5,775.00
F.	Electricity	600.00	680.00
G.	Property Taxes	3,120.00	3,120.00
H.	Insurance	1,320.00	1,320.00
I.	Miscellaneous Services		
	1) Accounting	600.00	560.00
	2) Legal	360.00	380.00
	3) Pest Control	240.00	240.00
J.	Security	1,200.00	1,210.00
	TOTAL	$26,640.00	$27,110.00

II. Income

A.	Assessments from Owners	$35,208.00
B.	Interest Income	1,110.50
C.	1997 Surplus	88.00
	TOTAL	$36,406.50

ANNUAL FINANCIAL REPORT
FORM 13.62

III. **Summary**

A.	Total Income for Operations		$36,406.50
B.	Total Expenses for Operations		27,110.00
			9,296.50
C.	Total 1998 Collections -		
	Reserve Contributions		- 8,568.00
	SURPLUS		$ 728.50

IV.   **Capital Expenses And Deferred Maintenance**

		Painting	Pool	Roof	Misc
A.	Beginning Balance	$ 9,216.00	$ 1,200.00	$ 6,000.00	$ 720.00
B.	1998 Collections	4,608.00	600.00	3,000.00	360.00
C.	Interest Earned	812.00	77.00	512.00	57.50
D.	1998 Expenditures	0.00	1,750.00	0.00	256.00
BALANCE AT YEAR END		$ 14,636.00	$ 127.00	$ 9,512.00	$ 881.50

ANNUAL FINANCIAL REPORT (cont.)
FORM 13.62

CLAIM OF LIEN
BY
THE ESTATES HOMEOWNERS ASSOCIATION, INC.

STATE OF FLORIDA)
COUNTY OF PINELLAS)

In accordance with the authority of the Declaration of Covenants and Restrictions of the Association, THE ESTATES HOMEOWNERS ASSOCIATION, INC., hereby claims a lien for all unpaid homeowners association assessments now delinquent and hereafter accrued against the property and the owner described below, in the initial amount and from the date stated, together with interest and reasonable attorney's fees and costs incident to the collection hereof, as follows:

		AMOUNT OF
OWNER	DUE DATE	ASSESSMENT
MARC MATTHEW	July 1, 1997	$39.78

Property Description

Lot 1, Block 10, THE ESTATES SUBDIVISION, according to the map or plat thereof recorded in Plat Book 91, Pages 7 through 12, Public Records of Pinellas County, Florida.

DONE AND EXECUTED this 15th day of August, 1997.

                          THE ESTATES HOMEOWNERS
                          ASSOCIATION, INC.

(CORPORATE SEAL)   By: _____
                                    President
ATTEST:

_____

Secretary

On this 15th day of August, 1997, personally appeared the President and Secretary of The Estates Homeowners Association,

CLAIM OF LIEN
FORM 13.63

Inc., and acknowledged that they executed this Claim of Lien for the purposes therein expressed.

_____
Notary Public

My commission expires:

SATISFACTION OF LIEN
BY
THE ESTATES HOMEOWNERS ASSOCIATION, INC.

STATE OF FLORIDA)
COUNTY OF PINELLAS)

FOR AND IN CONSIDERATION of a valuable sum in dollars, receipt of which is hereby acknowledge, the undersigned releases the lien recorded in Official Records Book 1000, Page 100, Public Records of Pinellas County, Florida, from the property owned by MARC MATTHEW and described as follows:

> Lot 1, Block 10, THE ESTATES SUBDIVISION, according to the map or plat thereof recorded in Plat Book 91, Pages 7 through 12, Public Records of Pinellas County, Florida.

DONE AND EXECUTED this 30th day of August, 1997.

THE ESTATES HOMEOWNERS
ASSOCIATION, INC.

(CORPORATE SEAL)   By: _____
                                          President
ATTEST:

_____
Secretary

On this 30th day of August, 1997, personally appeared the President and Secretary of The Estates Homeowners Association, Inc., and acknowledged that they executed this Satisfaction of Lien for the purposes therein expressed.

_____
Notary Public

My commission expires:

SATISFACTION OF LIEN
FORM 13.64

INDEX

160

YES! Please send Mr. Dunbar's *The Homeowners Association Manual (Third Edition)*

Name _____

Address _____

City _____ State _____ Zip _____

Qty	Title	@	Total
	The Homeowners Assocation Manual	$18.50*	

*Price includes sales tax, shipping and handling

Send order and check to: SUNCOAST PROFESSIONAL
PUBLISHING CORPORATION
P.O. Box 10094
Tallahassee, Florida 32302

YES! Please send Mr. Dunbar's *The Homeowners Association Manual (Third Edition)*

Name _____

Address _____

City _____ State _____ Zip _____

Qty	Title	@	Total
	The Homeowners Assocation Manual	$18.50*	

*Price includes sales tax, shipping and handling

Send order and check to: SUNCOAST PROFESSIONAL
PUBLISHING CORPORATION
P.O. Box 10094
Tallahassee, Florida 32302

CUT ALONG LINES